SKEEM LIFE

SKEEM LIFE

Growing up in the Seventies

Gary Robertson

BLACK & WHITE PUBLISHING

First published 2010
by Black & White Publishing Ltd
29 Ocean Drive, Edinburgh EH6 6JL

1 3 5 7 9 10 8 6 4 2   10 11 12 13

ISBN: 978 1 84502 321 8

Typeset by Iolaire Typesetting, Newtonmore
Printed and bound by MPG Books Ltd, Bodmin

CONTENTS

To my Mum and Dad
who gave me the happiest childhood
anyone could wish for

ACKNOWLEDGEMENTS

This book would never have been written without the inspiration from a fellow Dundee writer and friend Wullie Robertson. It wasn't until I read his fabulously funny debut book *On The Milk*, about life as a Dundee milkboy in the early '60s, that the idea for *Skeem Life* came about. A million thanks Wullie!

Eternal thanks to my parents John and Margaret Robertson and my sister Steff for the 'best family home in the world'! To my beautiful wife Sue and precious children Cailean and Eilidh for supporting me and letting me off with doing the ironing and the dishes for six months while I wrote this. I owe you all one.

Thanks also to all my family and friends, the ones who have passed (especially my late grandparents Nobby and Bett) and those still here, for believing in me and supporting me – it really does mean the world to me. To Campbell and all at Black & White Publishing for sticking with me and allowing the masses to read my work.

And lastly, this book is an extended dedication to the fowk o the Dundee hoosin skeemz. The strong and proud working class people I grew up with, who shared the laughs and at times tears, but always came out the other side with smiles on their faces and warmth in their hearts. I may get labelled a 'big Jessie' for this but I love you all. Thanks.

SKEEM LIFE

Skeem life, itz the only life eh ken
Skeem life, standin in the pishin ren
Skeem Life, gittin doag shite on yir shoes
Skeem life, throwin stanes at gulls an doo's

Weer the fowk wah grew, fae the tenement slums
Often labelled common, sometimes branded scum
Ken wut tho? Wih wir happy as fuck!
Wih played the only weh wih kent, up tih wir ears in muck
Fishin fir flookeez aff the Broughty Ferry pier
Lissnin tih the sing-sangz in yir grannie's at New Year
Aw fir fuck sake, no the Wild Rover again
Wiv been hearin that shite fir years, thir must be sumhin else yih ken

Skeem life, itz the only life eh ken
Skeem life, is it ingin? Is it plehn?
Skeem life, sittin on a berry bus
Skeem life, gittin sna ba's in the pus

Skiffyin chuckies doon the Burnie, splashin throo muddy dubz
In an oot the bookeez an the boozer, spongin aff fowk fir a sub
Gittin blootird right oot yir tree, Monday moarninz on the seeck
Ach, uhv got some DIY tih dae, fuck it – uhl tak the week!
Fowk workin fir the minimum wage, ither fowk on the dole
The stull git beh, thirz nae silver spoon, life's nivir been a stroll
Queuin fir a white-puddin supper, any broken wafers aff the ice-cream van?
Plunderin aippuhlz aff posh fowk, waatchin fights wi' the Huns an the Shams

Skeem life, itz the only life eh ken
Skeem life, up at Tannadice or Dens
Skeem life, spam an chips an beans fir tea
Skeem life, waitin on a 33

Sure sometimes itz rough, yih see it ah in the skeemz
Some fowk fa beh the wayside, nivir realehz thir dreams
But ehl tell yih thirz some REAL talent there
Thirz a wealth o youthful energy, jist lookin fir the chance tih share
Musicians, futba players, singers, actresses as well
An a thoozand ithers like thum, wi' ither gifts tih sell
Itz the same in any city, wih share familiar stories
This is jist OOR street culture, telt in language we ca OARY!

Skeem life, itz the only life we've kent
Skeem life, sometimes nivir pyed wir rent
Skeem life, itz wahr oor herts uhl ayewiz be
Skeem life – the hoosin skeemz o oor Dundee!

1

TENE-MENTAL LIFE

Before the brand new estates arrived in Dundee, most of us lived in the old tenements. Home for my family was a dilapidated old tenement in Ryehill Lane, just off the Perth Road in the city's West End and that was where I soon established myself, after my arrival on 21 February 1967, as a 'right wee greetin-pussed whinger wah constantly mumped an girned'. Not that I remember much about it but that's what I've been told by my mum and dad.

Conditions in our tenement weren't great and the facilities, particularly the communal outside toilet – or lavvie as we knew it – left a lot to be desired. For my mum this was a constant complaint and she had some very close calls, especially trying to find the lav on pitch-black winter nights. It was more of an inconvenience than a convenience.

Life in the knackered old tenement was definitely pretty basic in the late '60s. We were all very close, literally, but sometimes a wee bit too close for comfort. My dad told me about a loud argument he and my mum once had after a big night out which ended up, without any real malice intended, with him pushing her. Mum stumbled backwards into a window and it smashed on impact. The raised voices and sound of crashing glass startled the woman downstairs who shouted up, 'Hey, wull yih keep the bliddee noise doon up there!'

With a few pots of foaming ale down his gullet the old man felt brave enough to reply, 'Ach, shut yir pus an mind yir ane business!'

'Dinna you talk tih me like that. Ehl send mih man up!'

'Ach send uhm up, ehl be here.'

What he really should have said at the beginning of the conversation was, 'Oh, ehm affy sorry aboot the noise, ehl git that gless swept up right away Mrs J,' but Dutch courage had meddled in the proceedings and placed him right in the shite! The family below were well known to my parents and well known in the city as people not to get on the wrong side of. The males were all of the 'built-like-a-brick-shithouse' type whose arguments were usually solved with a clenched fist like an anvil cracking you in the pus. Then they asked the questions but the unconscious bodies never replied. Shortly after the smash the inevitable knock on the door came. My old man opened it to find one of the sons filling the entire space of the door frame.

'Mih mither wizna too happy at the weh yih spoke tih ir.' The fact that there was any dialogue at all was a good sign, something which my old man could possibly work on, to save his face from being rearranged.

By this time the drink-fuelled bravado had deserted him: 'Oh eh didna mean tih upset yir mither like that son. Wih wir jist haein a wee argument an the windee accidentally smashed an ehm affy sorry an it'll no happen again.'

Luckily, the apology worked and the son returned downstairs and the proposed trip to the DRI (Dundee Royal Infirmary) was called off.

The smashed window had created a big problem though and thoughts soon turned on how to get it fixed. There was only one man for the job so dad called his brother-in-law, my uncle

Andy, to assist. Andy had tools, he had knowledge and he also had an advanced degree in skulduggery. In simple terms he was a very likeable 'fleh man' (fly man) who had been trained in the underground art of being fleh by his mate, who was a master fleh man. One of their ingenious little earners was to join a 'Clubbie book' where you could order goods then pay the company back in instalments. What the fleh men did was have the goods delivered to a bogus address, usually an empty house and make sure they were in when the delivery arrived or have them left with a neighbour, then they'd simply disappear with the haul. They argued that they were just 'borrowing' the goods on a long term basis – very long – but I don't believe they had a plan in place to return them!

One of the items obtained on the fleh was an early and very primitive version of a sun lamp for getting a homemade suntan. It sat in a tin box and when plugged in, two angled metal rods, similar to welding rods, made a bridging connection and produced a blinding ultraviolet light. The rods went red hot and would slowly burn down which, in turn, eventually led to the connection being lost. The whole contraption had no insulation and on many occasions Andy and my old man nearly melted their hands when trying to adjust the rods. The instructions recommended wearing the little safety goggles to protect the eyes and sitting a 'safe distance' from the light.

'Ach bugger that John,' said Uncle Andy. 'Wull sit right up close tih it an git tanned quicker.'

'Maks sense Andy, you hae furst shot then ehl tak meh turn. Wull be lookin like bronzed Greek gods in nae time.'

'Here, meh pus feels like itz on fire! The sweat's lashin aff is!'

'Geez the goggles here an ehl hae a wee shot.'

After a while, the 'bronzed Greek gods' statement was

looking a bit wide of the mark – they were more like two 'scarlet Dundee numpties' with white circles around their eyes! There was only one way to combat this so they got shot of the goggles and got their non-tanned eyes even closer.

The old man said, 'Efter yid done yir shift yih couldna see a bliddee thing, ahin wiz jist pure white. Yid treh an fit the new rods an burn yir hands aff. Christ knows wut damage wih done tih wir skin. It wiz like sittin wi' yir face twa inches fae the sun! Eh sade tih Andy, "Is that no runnin awa wi' a load o electricity?" Ee jist laughed an shook eez hade as if tih say, "Ir you daft?"'

Back then, 'free electricity' was commonplace among many households, another of the fleh man's tricks. One way to sort this was to file a piece from an old vinyl record down and slot it into the meter far enough to stop the wheel clocking up units and ultimately – debt. When the wheels stopped running, the scheme folk's hot bath taps began turning, the four rings went on the cookers as did just about every other electrical appliance in the house. It was a luxury that didn't cost a penny and it was a wee result for the peasantry.

Meantime, the broken window still had to be fixed: 'Right John, wut wull dae is go up tih the aald hooses an tak a windee frame an wih should be able tih jist slot it in.'

'Sounds like a plan Andy.'

So off they went and got a frame which looked about the same size. What they hoped to do was simply replace the damaged one but unfortunately, it didn't match. Time for Plan B. After a painstakingly long few hours they had managed to carefully chip off the hard putty and take the pane out but this didn't fit either.

'Dinna worry John, ehv got the gless cutter here. Huv yih got the new putty riddee?'

'Oh eh.'

Andy then took my old man through a long and detailed explanation on the do's and don't's of glass cutting with an expertly delivered seminar. His apprentice listened intently, soaking up all this valuable advice.

'Now ah wih dae is mak one smooth score, jist one mind, gie it a dunt an Boab's yir uncle!'

Dunt. Smash. 'BUGGER!' The air went blue with a volley of profanities. All their hard and patient labour gubbed at the stroke of a dunt! The hilarious bit about it was they went and performed the exact same operation on a fresh frame only to smash it at the same critical moment! After a whole day's labour they finally managed to mend the window on their third attempt. It was a long, long time after before they saw the funny side of it though.

My only regret (if I could call it that) was that I wasn't born just that little bit earlier and have some memories of the tenement life. Stories abound from the older generation of tough but happy times which did indeed have aspects of 'mental' thrown in. For a great many though, including my own family, life was about to change completely.

2

A HOOSE IN THE CLOUDS

Like I say, I don't have any memories of staying in the Ryehill Lane tenement as we moved to the brand new housing scheme of Whitfield sometime in 1969. Many of Britain's housing schemes sprung up after the Second World War as cities tried to recover from the effects of a hellish tit-for-tat bombing campaign. Another reason forcing this regeneration and outward growth was the huge problem of overcrowding that had blighted many of the country's city centres. In Dundee, it was reported that living conditions, overcrowding and squalor were second only to Glasgow, as far as Scotland was concerned.

Whitfield had been built in the 1960s so, when we moved there it was still nearly new. However, this state-of-the-art scheme with its pioneering Skarne buildings quickly went downhill and the area became rough as hell and no coz we moved there!

We settled into our new life nine storeys up in one of the two huge multi blocks. Ours was called Whitfield Court and the other was Murrayfield Court. The building of these 'communities in the sky' had gained popularity throughout many cities during the '60s but they were an experiment that just didn't work. Although the correct term for our new dwelling was a flat we always referred to it as our house or 'hoose'.

For my family (especially mum!) though and countless

others no doubt, the real pleasure was the inside lavvie. Money wasn't always available for luxuries like toilet roll and sometimes pages from the *Tully* or *Courier* newspapers had to be used, not so good with their sharp, folded corners. My old man, whose DIY was to become legendary, not to mention a great money saver, patented an early scheme 'bog roll hudder'. This consisted of a block of wood with a metal rod fixed in the middle onto which a pile of neatly torn squares of last night's paper were placed. It never really took off across the rest of the city as far as I'm aware but it worked brilliantly in oor hoose.

My old man was full of great ideas and also decided to decorate my new bedroom with a huge painted clown on the wall which used to stare at me at bed time. *Chucky* (of horror film fame) was still a good eighteen or so years away from our screens but this forefather of dolls and clowns was doing an excellent job of scaring the wits out of me every night. As the last stroke of paint left the brush my mum appeared and said, 'Aw, thatz bra John, the bairn's gonna feel right at hame wi' that on the wah.'

'Oh eh yir spot on there, Mum, ehm gonna be wettin the bed ivree night an cha'in on the puhllay under the blankets! Yih canna bate a good nightmare.'

Rooms were heated by convectors blowing out hot air but weren't on that often as they cost an absolute fortune to run. By the time my wee sister Steff appeared on the scene late in 1969, the money had to stretch even further so the hoose was even colder.

Money was always tight in those days. The old man worked in the 'Sosh' – CWS jute mill off Arbroath Road – and he was soon joined by my mum doing some extra shifts while we were looked after by babysitters. Usually though we were looked after by my gran and granda Clark who lived in the neighbouring scheme of Fintry.

As a child, none of those adult issues of hardship and financial worries bothered you. All that mattered was having fun and these concrete jungles were just one great big adventure. These were the days before do-gooders with the personalities of mannequin dummies on Valium were allowed to wrap the world in cotton wool and we as kids were able, and indeed encouraged, to roam with carefree abandon. There were many occasions when the lift was knackered and you'd have to hike up the nine flights of stairs, sometimes in total darkness when the lights had been panned in. These days that would be considered way too dangerous but for us it was the norm.

Some landings you passed would have anything from dog or human excrement or pish or a mix of all them. This delightful spectacle was usually complimented with artwork from the local creative literati whose work adorned walls, ceilings and floors alike with spray-painted classics such as 'YOUNG SHAMS RULE YA BASS' sitting proudly in the centre of the gallery. Vandalism and open toilets were accepted and we as bairns never batted an eyelid.

You were always encouraged to 'git oot an play' by your parents and, virtually from the moment you were on your feet, you were out and about sussing out the surroundings. We were really only toddlers but this process was an important step to becoming streetwise. The further you wandered the more familiar you became with the area. We'd travel as far as Tarzie's (Tarzan's) Island on the outskirts of the scheme which was a real adventure although in all my visits there I never once saw a guy swinging through the trees, screaming like he'd just sat on a rusty tent pole with only a wee piece of material keeping him decent! It was, in fact, just a hill covered in bushes but it offered excellent hidey-holes for playing games on, way before they plonked Whitfield High School onto part of it.

I can always remember playing at the foot of the multis and thinking they were toppling over. This, of course, was nonsense and was caused by the clouds moving above but it still felt real as a bairn. With the scheme still very much in the process of being developed, there wasn't much in the way of set entertainment. There were a couple of swing parks and a few climbing frames dotted around, one of these being a fire engine which I used to love playing on. Some were very basic though and had as much thought and creativity put into them as a bairn filling its nappy! It was much more fun climbing trees, walls and buildings and playing on the mounds of earth left by digger trucks. After a good rainfall there seemed to be an abundance of dubs (puddles) to splash in but the biggest one I ever saw (and played in) was near the foot of our multi. This stretch of water formed a new loch in the scheme and naturally, became a magnet for all the kids.

One day I was having a wee paddle in the shallow part when some big laddie came along and lobbed one of my sandals away out into the middle of 'Loch Whitfield' where it sank out of sight. With no chance of retrieving it I made my way up the nine flights of stairs, crying my wee heart out to tell my mum of my loss. She probably gave me a good slap for being so stupid and being in there in the first place.

The swing parks were pretty basic affairs usually consisting of a few swings, a roundabout, seesaw and the obligatory crap climbing frame. The park designers must have been a real sadistic breed back then because all the surfaces were made of bone-breaking stone and there was no shortage of kids to put this to the test. Almost every visit would result in an injury to someone. Most dangerous of all was the seesaw which had the uncanny ability of pinging lighter kids off like ragdolls and smashing them onto the hard surface. In saying that, a fall from a climbing frame could be just as painful, especially if the first point of contact was a bar between the legs! Older boys used to 'bronco' the swings which meant standing up on them, then leaping off, kicking at the same time so that the swing would go wrapping around the frame thus rendering it useless. Occasionally, youngsters would get cracked on the head or under the chin as they walked innocently by. Thinking back, usually it was safer playing on shop roofs or climbing over barbed wire than playing in these parks.

At home, our TV was black and white and occasionally needed a good thump to clear the blizzard from the picture. There was no way we could afford a phone but if something was that important and a call was needed then Mum or Dad would take a 2p piece or a 10p (two bob but) and use the public phone box down on the street. One luxury we did have was an ancient portable record player which sat in a big wooden case where you simply lifted the lid to play. 'Portable' was a bit wide of the mark though as this thing weighed a bloody ton. It was decorated with paper in a wood grain effect which seemed slightly daft considering it was made of wood. This fake wood look was also available in wallpaper form which we eventually got, possibly to match the record player.

Like most people we never had a washing machine so my old lady had to book a slot in the laundry on the ground floor. From there the washing would be hung out in the huge communal drying area under the multi but sometimes things would get nicked off the line by some chancer. This practice was known as 'snowdropping' and many occasions I remember my mum going nuts when a pair of the old man's jeans or a jumper or shirt had been lifted.

As I say money was tight and it didn't help when the old man decided he was going to be the next Bob Dylan and went out and bought a guitar for twenty quid from Forbes' music shop in King Street. Twenty quid back then was equivalent to about five hundred pounds these days! Of course he didn't have a spare twenty quid and as was the norm at the time he took it 'on tick' and payed in instalments. This was sometimes referred to as the 'never never plan' due to the high interest rate on the repayment and lack of funds where the item was never, never going to be finally paid off.

With mum struggling to put grub on the table and threatening to put the guitar 'ower eez napper', he argued that he could get involved in the thriving 'folk circuit' and make some good money. In reality, what happened was he hammered out some woeful backing chords for his mates who *could* play, and he pished any profits against the urinals of the Chrome Rail bar at the bottom of Peter Street. Mum? Needless to say she was ecstatic with this visionary set up and backed him all the way in his burgeoning musical career.

Incidentally, this infamous bar which was occasionally frequented by hard men and brawlers was where my old man got offered 'ootside fir a square go', probably by some disgruntled customer taking umbrage at his terrible chord changes with the band. Not a fighting man by any means, he decided he wasn't taking this nonsense and put his pint down then went outside to sort the antagonist out.

He knew how to talk the 'street talk' from working in the jute mills and opened with the classic, 'C'mon then yih prick!' Unfortunately his focus was on the prick and he didn't notice a smaller prick (who was mates with the original prick) charge in, pick him up by the lapels of his bottle green velvet jacket and throw him right through the D.E.C.S. (Dundee Easten Co-operative Shop) window. He lay there sprawled on a pile of glass, half in the shop and half out, with a huge piece of plate glass dangling precariously above his legs.

'Wut happened there?' he thought as the two pricks bolted up the pendie. He managed to crawl out before being guillotined and going home more legless than he already was, and was off before the polis arrived. Following a good old stagger he fell into a phone box in the Thorter Row pendie (this was situated off the High Street near where the present Primark shop is in the new Overgate Centre) and tried to phone a taxi. After many unsuccessful attempts he fell back out the door with the phone still in his hand and when the door shut on him he lost the plot and yanked the phone from its wire. Details are sketchy as to whether he kept trying to phone after this but it ended up back in the multi with him.

Putting the sober head on he entered the house and climbed into bed, rather chuffed that he'd escaped without a roond o the guns for being blootered. The roond o the guns saved itself for the morning when he was placed in front of the firing squad. As he awoke from his drunken stupor he felt wetness below him and instantly thought he'd pished the bed. It wasn't that serious however, it was only blood and with mum's curses ringing in his ears he made his way up to the DRI (Dundee Royal Infirmary) to have his arse stitched back up.

Looking back now, my old man was probably the reason why credit cards became so popular in the years to come. If he saw something he wanted he sure as hell was having it. Buy now and worry about payments later. Of his many 'must have' purchases the best one was most definitely a cine film camera.

A HOOSE IN THE CLOUDS

In 1971 a lot of folk didn't even possess a basic run-of-the-mill snapshot camera and here was my old man running about like an extra from Universal Studios in a housing scheme. Although my mum was going to brain him at the time for buying anither load o shite, this extravagant piece of equipment was to provide a historical record of the next fifteen Christmas and summer holidays.

3

CRIME AND PUNISHMENT

As a child I was never one for thieving (thankfully it's stayed that way!) but one day my need for sweets got the better of me and I became a young criminal. It wasn't long after Britain had gone decimal in 1971 and changed from the old monetary system, so I would have been about five years old at the time. My dad's pay packet was kept on the living room windowsill for some reason and I went into it and took a pound note from it. At that tender age I must have been (for that day anyway!) the richest five-year-old in Whitfield and possibly all the other schemes in Dundee as well. This was an outrageous amount of dough to have. When the lift reached the ground floor and I stepped outside into the shadow of the towering multi, there was still no sign of my mum screaming at me. That was when I knew I was about to enter 'sweetie heaven'.

When you consider you could buy two *Black Jacks* or two *Fruit Salads* for a half pence then I could have had filled pockets the size of Royal Mail bags in my shorters and still had dough left over. I distinctly recall ordering loads of sweets and handing the money over only to be handed back about 77p. I was *still* loaded and began to really panic, mind you not before I waded in about the pile of sweets which I had no way of finishing in a month of Sundays.

CRIME AND PUNISHMENT

I suspect I spread the money wisely over the coming year as my horrendously devious action was never uncovered. I could just imagine my poor dad defending himself courageously and protesting his innocence against my mum's accusations, 'Thirz a pound missin oot o here. Yoov musta pished it against the wah. Well yih better bliddee dae some overtime an mak that back up again, ehm waarnin yih!'

There was no way that was ever going to happen though as more often than not my old man followed a Great British tradition back then and only worked a four-day week. This was sometimes extended to a three-day and in extreme cases a two-day week. Monday was part of the 'Bombay Fast' and was viewed by many workers as a recovery day following the weekend's swallyin! Occasionally, he did partake in a bit of overtime but he never actually did the time. At the back of five, he'd perform a bit of limbo and wriggle out the lavvie window and off up the road, happy in the knowledge he was being paid until 7.30.

My mum had her own wee sideline for swelling the family income to somewhere just above 'skint' and worked as a sales executive for the globally recognised company Tupperware. To put it in its proper housing scheme context, she was a kind of female Arthur Daley who went to parties in houses filled with a load o babblin weemin and tried to sell them various items of shite from a huge case. Tupperware must have had the monopoly on some hidden plastic mountain in the heart of 'Plasticland' and proceeded to make measuring jugs, bowls, plates and re-sealable containers knowing that these women would be slavering at the mouth to buy them and fill every space in their kitchens with them.

This practice was worked between other sellers on a 'you

host a perty fir me an ehl hae ane fir you' basis. Family members, work colleagues and neighbours would turn up and await the arrival of a fellow female Arthur Daley who'd drag in her bulging case and fill our living room with a ton of plastic junk. That was then the cue to get ladled in about the Cinzano Bianco and Babycham and the high pitched cackling and screeching decibel level would then increase to epic proportions. Me and my wee sister were, of course, sent to bed and told to 'git tih sleep!'

'Wut? Ir you bein serious mither? Yiv got a banshee's convention ragin through the hoose wi' "Son Of My Father" batterin oot on the record player an yoor waantin us tih go tih *sleep?* NAE DANGER!' It was time to have a right carry on and when that got boring we'd keep running up the loabee and into the party.

'Wull you twa git tih sleep afore eh skelp yir bliddee erses! Now, sorry Helen, as eh wiz sayin, the salt an pepper set come in at 52p an ehl throw in a plastic ashtray as well, howz that?'

The only reason we were able to create mayhem for a sustained period was that the old man was oot the hoose and probably doing another sell out gig in The Chrome Rail or we would have got a right leatherin! These were the good old days when a good tanking for being a pain in the arse was accepted as the norm and indeed was expected. Most bairns were in the same boat and it was a tradition that was passed down through the generations. It was done to let you know just who the boss was when you tried pushing the boundaries and like I say, it was accepted. It must be stressed however that this discipline was not to be confused with the barbaric variety which some poor folk had to deal with. Our punishments had different levels depending on the crime committed or if the old man had got a knock back for some hanky panky with the old lady:

Light Punishment
THE CUFF
This was applied, usually by the old man with the open hand who'd flick it at speed, catching the back of the nut and jolting it forward. The pain level wasn't too bad but it did have a shock value. This was a reminder to watch your step and was dealt out for offences ranging from spilling your juice on the lino, minor cheek (talking back to your elders), clypin (grassing), bouncing on the settee or not eating your tea.

More Light Punishment
THE SLAP
This was solely the old lady's domain. Again, this had an open hand application and could be served up on most parts of the body. The face cheeks were taboo but occasionally rules were flouted for a good 'slap in the pus'. The obvious area was the arse but my mum's personal favourite was the legs, especially when shorters were worn. Holding one of your hands for leverage which also cut off any means of escape, she'd catch the back of the unprotected leg or legs and leave a burning red hand print. Depending on the offence this action could be repeated as often as the striker felt necessary. In most cases the latter was performed in a frenzy when PMT was involved as well. More often than not, these blows were dished out for sustained girning and were painful. Being dragged around Littlewoods while mither tried to decide whether to buy a pund o mince or sliced polony and distracting her with heavy girning was only going to produce one outcome. There was never a warning 'Cuff' before 'The Slap'.

Medium Punishment

THE BOOT UP THE ERSE

This was favoured solely by the old man (as without adequate protection from open-toed furry slippers, the old lady would probably have broken her big toe!) and was dished out for various offences of a more serious nature including getting nabbed playing chickenelly on neighbours' letterboxes, getting a bad report from school, or drawing pictures of malformed dinosaurs on the new wallpaper with crayons. The pain level from this strike could be anything from quite sair to makkin yih greet like anyhing!

Brutal Punishment

THE WAHLUP OR SKELP

This was definitely the most serious one of them all and could be administered by both parents, although not together I may add! Two names for the same strike and both equally devastating. When the previous three were having no effect or the offence outstripped lesser ones by a long way, the Wahlup was unleashed. This was a versatile strike using the front or back of the hand and applied at high speed and with force. The whole body was fair game and the pain was of the numbing variety. Depending on how far the offender had gone the striker would sometimes see fit to dish out another Wahlup and in extreme cases may even throw in a Cuff, a Slap and Boot up the Erse for good measure. Any weak signs of crying and howling with pain were met with threats of, 'Wut ir yih greetin fir? Ehl gie yih sumhin tih greet aboot in a minit!'

This statement always threw me as it was quite obvious what I was greetin for. I'd just been assaulted with parental love in the name of discipline. 'Git tih yir bliddee bed!' usually followed the Wahlup and if the offence was carried out in the early afternoon, you had a hellish long day and night ahead. Experimenting for the first time with your mum's lighter, putting the house keys in the bin or skiffying Tupperware lids out the window were all deemed Wahlupable offences.

There were added bonuses, of course, for my mum as a Tupperware seller. The more crap you could fob off on victims, the more crap Tupperware fobbed off on you as a 'thank you'. We had the only house in Whitfield Court with 85% plastic accessories ranging from items such as a plastic toaster, a plastic ironing board and a plastic dartboard. Slight exaggeration but one of my favourite perks of the Tupperware era was the homemade ice-lolly makers. This innovative invention did away with the need for the hugely scarce cash which would have bought a top of the range *Lyons Maid* number and instead, only required some orange concentrate and a steady hand. I only ever remember there being orange juice, not like nowadays when you can have Californian cranberry and cask-conditioned kiwi, Hungarian Peach Melba and rusted prune or pinewood cinnamon resin and pomegranate dew drop flavours. What the hell happened?

The passage of time is lost on a child and as soon as the juice was poured in, the inevitable, 'Is it riddee yit mum?' eagerly followed. As soon as she was out the room you were in the freezer checking. Once it *was* ready the plastic cap was removed revealing a 'pure orange' ice-lolly held by the ingenious plastic stem. This was all fine and well and tasted great until the concentrate started running low and was rationed much more thinly. The ice-lollies then took on the appearance of ice that had been peed on giving it a slightly 'coloured' look and tasted as lame as it looked.

In keeping with the Tupperware theme, there's the memory

of another plastic classic – the milk sachet holder. Some boffin with too many O Levels had come up with the great idea of putting milk into plastic bags. The idea was you cut a small piece from both corners of the sachet, placed it in the holder and poured at a measured forty-five-degree angle. In reality what happened was that we as bairns would finish one sachet, go and get the scissors and cut a corner from the back-up sachet which usually did away with half the bag. The result was a pouring catastrophe as a tidal wave of milk washed Rice Krispies, mugs, chairs, cats and everything else that wasn't nailed down, out into the landing. The only action following this type of accident was the Wahlup! The ironic thing is, nearly forty years after acquiring some of these items my mum still uses them on a daily basis to this day. So it couldn't have all been crap!

4

JR'S AN FASHION NEEDS

As a bairn, fashion was about as relevant as a cow dropping a large cowpat on a bumblebee's head in a field. Your mum bought, acquired, nicked or received hand-me-down clothes which she put on you and you happily went out to play in. Scheme life certainly didn't provide the ideal arena for a budding fashionista or catwalk wannabe. Everyone was in the same boat – we were minks, although I use that term loosely as the word itself could be used in many guises. Behaviour such as eating an old sweet which was lying in the street (a pickie aff the grund) or picking your nose and eating a doolie (crusted snot) could get you labelled as a 'mink' as would the wearing of a pair of wellies when the sun was splitting the pavements. Like I say, the way you were dressed meant you were a kind of mink especially if you were stood next to say, someone who went to Dundee High or who came from Broughty Ferry.

Our brand of minkiness however was not to be confused with the *real* mink. This was a person or persons whose house resembled that of a shitehouse. The kind of dwelling that looked like a herd of elephants had run through and shat in it at the same time. It stunk and so did the inhabitants. Haein a waash was definitely way down the list of priorities for this unique breed of human beings.

As a one-bath-a-week boy, like many of my peers, we could consider ourselves dead clean compared to the real minks. With bath night being on a Sunday any days-old engrained dirt which had accumulated throughout the week on the ankles, knees, hands and elbows or tide marks around the neck was simply washed away with a spit and a rub from a sleeve. Some bath nights were particularly painful affairs when my mum stepped into her role of do-it-yourself 'hairdresser'. She had one of those plastic hair trimmers (made famous by Billy Connolly) which she used to keep me and my sister's hair down to a controllable level, thus saving money on barbers and hairdressers costs. I'm sure she bought it from a shop that dealt in weapons of torture. This barbaric item of pain should never have been on sale and should in fact have been banned as a weapon of mass destruction under the Geneva Convention!

The device itself was a little flat piece of plastic with two ends of combed teeth, each with a razor blade in them. One end had 'trim', the other had 'cut' when in fact they both should have said 'RIP!' All they did was tear clumps of your hair out from their roots and it was sore as hell. My old lady seemed to think the best time to perform the cut was after a bath while the hair was still wet. The screams and tears were ignored as she stroked over the hair with this implement of carnage. She'd have been as well just getting a pair of my old man's pliers and ripping it out with them! If parents used one of these on their kids nowadays they'd get done for GBH and locked up for six months.

When she'd finished there was no mirror like at the barbers to show you your new look – that would have been far too traumatic to witness. No, it was a case of 'stop yir greetin an git yirsel drehd, yir sister's nixt!' It was a good few years before my mum decided to give up the DIY hairdressing and I was never so glad to see the back of that horror tool and be taken for a proper haircut.

I should also say that my parents still have that same wee trimmer which caused so much terror and grief. We can laugh about it now but it sure wasn't funny at the time! Many years later when I was at Linlathen High School I went to the barbers and got a skinhead haircut. It was about a quarter inch long but when I got home I decided I wanted it shorter so I raked out the trimmer from the junk drawer and proceeded to skim over my napper with it. However, when I viewed my handy work in the mirror I nearly shat a brick. My head looked like it had been attacked with a machete. It was all streaked with different lengths and looked absolutely awful. There was no more money for another 'shorter' skinhead so I had to take the stick at school and wait on it growing back in.

It's fair to say that many folk look back at the 1970s and find themselves cringing at some of the fashions which did reach the streets. The arrival of Glam Rock must surely bear the brunt of most of the criticism for offloading a horrendous array of appalling gear onto the ordinary punters. The dawning of the new decade was heralded in by many of Britain's youth and young adults wearing the smart attire of the skinhead – mohair suits, Ben Sherman shirts, tonic Sta-Prest trousers and Crombie overcoats, etc. Granted there were still a load of hippies knocking about but sandals were never going to catch on in the snow and kaftan shirts made guys looks positively feminine especially when combined with long flowing locks.

Enter Marc Bolan, T-Rex and Co and everything went tits up. In the space of a relatively short time older youths in the schemes whom you considered to be quite hard were now parading around in lemon or turquoise Parallel trousers, four-inch platform shoes and wacky shirts with collars which could have taken off if they'd begun flapping. Suddenly these guys didn't look so hard any more.

I remember my mum had bought me this garment which was a kind of hybrid between a T-shirt and a polo shirt. It was made from part-cheesewire, part-electric shock inducing nylon and was about as comfortable as laying your head on a pillowcase filled with broken lightbulbs. After about three and a half minutes of wearing this thing, your nipples were sliced clean off. This was one of the 'dressier' items in my clothing range and mum would insist it was worn when I attended birthday parties or other official engagements. The fact that it was banned under the Cruelty to Children Act due to its torturous capabilities mattered nothing to her.

'Ach, yih look dead smart in that, eh shoulda got it in the rade stripes as well.'

'But mum, its affy itchy an it maks mih tits bleed.' *Slap! Slap!*

Honestly, it was like wearing a shirt made from fibreglass loft insulation and I was absolutely over the moon when the day came and it got too small to wear. My poor nipples felt exactly the same as I did and were finally able to heal, although they looked nothing like their pre-torture days. I only felt sorry for the poor laddie who was going to have to wear it after it was passed on to the Rag and Bone man.

For the record, the Rag and Bone man was some local scheme entrepreneur who would come round the streets in a battered old van blowing a trumpet or a whistle then shouting, 'Any aald rags?' On hearing this, us bairns would bother the lives out of our mums for a few items of old clothing or ask to take the bag she'd been saving up out to the van. The reward for this transaction was massive – a balloon! You didn't even get two for a bag full. It was standard rate across the board – one effin balloon! But off we went skipping, happy as Larry. I've no doubts there were some horror stories of parents having no old clothes to offer and their kids deviously taking an item or two from the chest of drawers of good gear, all for the sake of a measly balloon, but we *are* talking a *balloon* here!

For most kids sannayz (sandshoes) were the footwear of choice in the early '70s and if you were *really* lucky, you'd have a pair of basey's (baseball boots). These were the pre-Adidas, Nike, Bend-it-like-bloody-Beckham, 130 quid a pair days and were used for everything from playing football to climbing trees to runnin awa fae the 'Fuzz'. Surprisingly, for a thin piece of rubber and material they were able to take quite a hammering but one thing they weren't appropriate for was climbing harling walls. Their grip was second to none but after a few ascents up an doon a poley, the chuckies on the wall ripped the toes to shreds leaving two gaping holes and the threat o a good Wahlup fae yir mither.

Wellies were another favourite from that period and were largely acceptable, except as I said, when the sun was out. Sometimes though, this situation couldn't be helped as you'd head off to school in the morning and the rain was stotting down only for it to clear up a little later. Classmates knew the score on occasions like these which meant you were exempt from being tagged a mink. For boys who enjoyed a game of football, playing with these things on was a real nightmare. They afforded little if any control of the ball and when you did kick it, it was just a big *SKELP!* The same kind of noise you'd get if you slapped a fat lady's arse with a hot water bottle.

Whoever invented these wellies must have become an overnight millionaire as nearly all the kids in the schemes had a pair. I'm sure as hell certain however, that *they* didn't wear a pair of these bloody things on their *own* feet! They were about as useful as a rubber pole-vaulting stick and had the insulating capabilities of an igloo with no roof. In short, they were FREEZING! On top of that they had a comfort value of zero and your socks never stayed up long and would slide down and gather in the front of the boot. This created a painful problem when it rained as the rim of the wellies rubbed both your calves raw and made them weep. You always knew someone who'd suffered this affliction with the two red rings they were sporting on their legs. Obviously this problem was avoided if you had long trousers on but that wasn't character building at all.

The only thing wellies had going for them was that they were great for jumping in dubs. Their wading capabilities were minimal though, kids being kids, any judgement of deeper puddles or streams was non-existent and they simply lent themselves as water carriers when the cold water flooded over the tops. It's laughable to think that nowadays they have become a fashion accessory, especially at the big outdoor music festivals and people will pay ridiculous prices for the same useless rubber shite but which now have the 'all important' designer label on them.

With money being scarce, homemade clothing was an option open to those women who could knit. I don't know where my mum learned but she soon became a dab hand and was rattling off jumpers and tank tops and other accessories as she went into 'knit one, purl one' overdrive. Unfortunately for me and my sister, most of the items that came off her production line were made from wool which had the same itchy qualities as a pile of jaggy nettles. And woebetide you if you complained. The winter months were hellish as your mum happed you up and sent you out into a blizzard with the whole set on – jumper, scarf, balaclava and mitts attached with string. Add a bit of wellie rub and that was you set. The only thing that could have possibly made this any more uncomfortable was having a swarm of wasps stashed down your Y-Fronts!

Until very recently there was a shop in Dundee's Seagate area called JR's which was undoubtedly regarded as a Dundee institution, as familiar to the city as the Law Hill or the Old Steeple and a Mecca for housewives in particular who sought a wee bargain. The shop literally sold anything and everything and was packed from wall to wall with stuff, all ingeniously positioned in a space no bigger than a phone box. I don't know if it was coincidence or what but the shop's proprietor was called JR as well and he was a bit of a local footballing legend (for one half of the city anyway) during the mid-'50s, turning out for Dundee United and scoring a good few goals into the bargain. After hanging up his boots his entrepreneurial side shone through as he recognised the Dundee population's bizarre need to fill their houses with random stuff. There was no other shop in the town or the country where you could walk out with a pair of net curtains, a Showaddywaddy mirror and a watch which told you the time in Bangladesh while playing 'The Muckin' o Geordie's Byre'. The diversity of goods he stocked was legendary and many regulars agreed that some of it was even useful.

I remember my mum buying me my first ever digital watch from there which catapulted me into the higher echelon of pure cool among my wee band of mates. The old man must've had a Pool's win cause this thing cost about £1.75. Either that or my mum traded in her collection of 18,000 tokens from her fag packets for it.

While on that subject, fag packet tokens have to be one of the craziest Great British marketing ploys of the twentieth century. 'Yes folks, smoke like a chimney, fill yourselves with poisonous toxins which may see you into an early grave and we'll reward you with our exclusive tokens. If you're lucky to live long enough you can redeem your tokens with us. For 8,400 tokens you will get a lovely fish bowl. Or up your intake and 15,000 will get you our premium set of frosted glass ashtrays and for all you chain smokers out there, why not puff your way to our top offer of imitation silver lighter which includes a free tin of lighter fuel and all for just 24,750 tokens!'

As far as I'm aware JR never accepted fag tokens (or Green Shield Stamps for that matter!) and I was of course using creative poetic licence. However, my new watch was the dog's bollocks and I couldn't take my eyes off the red LED lights. This was something from the *future* and it was on *my* wrist. The fact I couldn't tell the damn time on it was irrelevant as I was totally hypnotised. My wee pals were amazed when I said, 'Here, check this oot lads, nae hands! Naw, the effin waatch yih clowns!'

'Aw, look at *that*. Is that a James Bond waatch?'

'Eh spot on, the very same. The signal beams doon fae sumwahr on the moon an lights it up see?'

'Aw . . .'

With their attention firmly set to 'awe' I turned up the descriptive dial on my new watch's powers. 'Eh, yih better waatch coz itz got a buhlt-in machine gun an a telescopic bazooka on it an ah.'

'Shite!'

'Eh?' I asked, totally shocked at this non-believer.

'Yir talkin shite. Meh auntie's got ane an itz wurked aff a wee battery thit goes in the back. C'mon lads, wir no listenin tih this pish any mair. Wahz waant a gemme o kick the can?'

And off they went, closely followed by a wee laddie wearing a no very special £1.75 digie waatch.

Another of my mum's early purchases from Dundee's first 'superstore' was a jacket she bought for me. But this was no *ordinary* jacket or poofy anorak. No, this was a combat soldier's parka, albeit for the six-year-old variety. These parkas were all the rage around 1972/73 and with JR having his finger on the retailing pulse he knew these were going to be a winner and loaded his shop up with them. If memory serves me right they were also available in navy but real soldiers wore the khaki green one. They had a bright red quilted lining, three drawstrings and loads of pockets for putting ammo like sandbombs and stones in.

Best feature of all though was the real fur hood. This fur looked suspiciously like cat fur and it wasn't until the later part of the decade when the jackets went out of fashion that the cat population in Britain began to increase in numbers again. Looking like an extra from the film *Ice Station Zebra* was all fine and well but the parka did have a couple of major drawbacks. Firstly, when soaked with rain it held more water than a pair of woolly swimming trunks and weighed a ton. Secondly, this wetness caused the jacket to stink like a camel's arse and suddenly, being an elite combat soldier wasn't so cool any more.

Unfortunately for the Dundonian masses, JR felt the need to evolve his entrepreneurial skills and recently ceased trading as JR. He opted for the new direction of a Glasgow Celtic FC souvenir shop which some in the city would argue sells much less attractive items than the original! For those who flocked to his shop in its heyday though, he remains a legendary and iconic figure in Dundee.

As for fashion, well that just got progressively worse. The

arrival of the Bay Shitty (sorry, City) Rollers on the music scene allegedly pushed tartan up to number one spot for trading on the World Stock Exchange as the planet went Roller daft. Tartan became a 'must have' accessory and was sown onto just about every conceivable item of clothing. Guys were now mincing about in half-mast lime green or scarlet Parallels with tartan gracing every seam. These could be matched with stripey pink and black Slade socks, double-decker Wedger shoes and Target shirts and Waster jumpers. My auntie Alice had hopped on the tartan bandwagon and became a massive Rollers fan after binning her David Cassidy posters. Being only a few years older than me she was a trendsetter in my eyes and I begged my mum to make me Rollers trousers like my auntie's. She eventually got some Royal Stewart tartan off the black market and sewed it up the seams of my trousers. The only problem was they were in a Prince of Wales dogtooth design and they looked absolutely horrendous with the red tartan. It was more like bad interference on a TV screen and my own Rollers bandwagon crashed into a ditch.

As a youngster I wouldn't eat bugger all so getting clothes to fit me was a big problem, especially trousers as my waist only measured around four inches in diameter. One pair of trousers I wished I could have worn from this period was called Patch Pockets. They were quite wide fitting with the main feature being the large pockets on the outside of the thighs. The problem was they were way lower than the standard hip pockets but this didn't stop the older 'cool' guys putting both their hands in them and walking like the Hunchback of Notre Dame. This was swaggering of the highest order and the ultra cool ones took it a step further and pushed their hands outwards, making the trousers enormous. Add a menacing scowl on the pus and these scheme gangsters were to be avoided at all costs. Some took this tough image to extreme levels and would place two bottles of lemonade in the pockets giving them a sinister gunslinger look.

Although they looked great, these trousers came with serious side effects on health such as bad posture and backache and it would be interesting to find out just how many of Dundee's present Zimmer frame users owe their problems to wearing Patch Pockets in the '70s.

5

EARLY HOLIDAYS

Skint as we were my parents felt it was important to try and provide a family holiday each summer even if it was just to escape the confines of the concrete jungle for a few days. For as long as I can remember the traditional summer holidays (the Dundee Fortnight as it's affectionately known) have been the last week in July and the first week in August. This was when the vast majority of the city's workers were off, unlike nowadays where there is so much more flexibility. Also, back then, most workers were paid weekly so when they came off for the Dundee Fortnight they had a weeks' wages plus their holiday pay which some guys went and pished against the nearest pub urinal and/or squandered in the bookies.

For many it was a great tradition to get steaming drunk before coming off on holiday. In the mills and factories the workers would have a 'burst up' (drink) before heading to the city's watering holes. On the whole this was accepted as working class culture and I'm sure most management turned a blind eye to their employee's final day bevvying. This seems laughable in the ultra-PC age we live in now where the workforce would probably be sacked on the spot.

On one such occasion my old man and his mate Larry had got themselves absolutely blootered in the mill. As they staggered their way home to Whitfield they were passing the Swanny Ponds when Larry said, 'Here John, c'mon wull git a fuckin boat each an hae a fuckin paddle roond the fuckin pond!' Larry as you may have noticed liked to stick a few sweary words into his vocabulary as he conversed. The guy was an absolute laugh-a-minute character and I used to love when he came up to visit because, for us as kids, this man used loads o 'bad words'. My mum however, would cringe. 'Larry, kin yih waatch yir language in front o the bairns?'

'Fuck sake Margaret, uhm sorry, eh didna fuckin ken eh wiz daein it!' You just couldn't fail to like him. He was practising sweary Tourette's way before it ever became fashionable and I'm sure if he'd met the Queen he'd have been exactly the same, 'Hullo Liz, how the fuck ir you doing? Itz fuckin great tih be in yir fuckin Highness's company. Oh fuck sorry, eh firgot tih fuckin bow, daft bastard!'

Back to the ponds and my old man thought a wee sail around would be a great idea. Both ponds in the Stobsmuir Park have long been a focal point for families to spend some leisure time either sailing model boats and fishing in the lower one or having a gentle row on the hired boats at the top pond. Alarm bells should have been ringing for the two drunks when they spotted two newly introduced Indian canoes. After paying the guy in the hut for an hour's sailing they both miraculously managed to get into the boats. However, disaster wasn't far away for the two wannabe Indian Braves. My old man paddled a distance of some five feet before the canoe tipped and he went straight into the three feet deep water. He stood up looking like the *Creature From The Black Lagoon* covered in black oily sludge. Of course Larry thought this was hilarious and was crying with laughter until the old man waded over and tipped him into the same sludge.

Their boating careers lay in tatters and after only two

minutes, both men soaked and dejected dragged their flooded vessels back to the shore. The parkie had watched this debacle unfold in front of his eyes and was not amused, 'Awa yih couple o eedeeits! Look it yiz, twa grown men? Yiz waant tih be ashamed o yirselz!'

Larry tried to make light of the situation and said, 'Fuckin sorry aboot that mate. Wir gonna go up the fuckin road an git cheenjed then come back coz wiv stull got fifty eight fuckin meenits' worth o sailin left!'

'Jist bugger off eh? Couple o pricks!'

They staggered over to Pitkerro Road and flagged a taxi down. When the driver got nearer though and saw two large pools of water at the men's feet and the state they were in, he put the foot down and took off. There was nothing else for it but to squelch home and face the music from their wives. I'm sure my dad must have got a severe bollocking but what I remember most was the pound notes and fivers hanging neatly on a wee makeshift washing line above the heater to dry out. Best of all though, mum had to pay the rent man that night and was totally mortified when she had to hand over the sodden notes.

My old man must have actually done a full week's work, either that or his career in the music business was taking off (I suspect it was the former!) for we had our first family summer holiday in 1970. Mum, dad, my baby sister and I boarded a train at Dundee's station and readied ourselves for the gruelling fifteen mile journey up the east coast to Arbroath. I think we just sat down and it was time to get off. We spent the week staying in a caravan at the famous Red Lion site. I don't remember much at all from that holiday except playing in the old outdoor swimming pool. Even though it was summer I'm sure my old man had to break the ice on the surface before

I got in to play, but we were made of tough stuff back then and you didn't take any notice of your body's core temperature dropping dangerously low.

The following two summers were spent away over on the west coast at the Butlins holiday camp in Ayr. The first time we travelled through via train and the second time we used the Bluebird bus from Dundee. This must have been utterly horrendous for my folks as kids travelling for any kind of distance are a nightmare. When you're wee, a journey to Ayr is like rowing to the southern end of Chile – the long way!

'Mum, ir wih there yit?'

'No! Wir only on Riverside Drehv so shut the hell up an eat yir Kelly an liquorice!'

As children we have no perception of time and distance and once the sweeties were finished the *real* mumpin an girnin started. My parents (and the rest of the bus) must have been well and truly demented by the time we got there. My memories of these years have been helped considerably by the footage my dad shot with his cine camera. The film was quite expensive so he'd save up for a 50ft reel each Christmas and summer then once he'd used it, it was sent off to be developed. Its arrival was always eagerly anticipated as we thought we were all film stars.

One hilarious piece of early footage nearly had my old man getting a thick ear from my mum. He was filming me and Steff playing at the bottom of the multis when he got momentarily distracted by a shapely redheaded woman who was passing by. The camera never lies as they say and the film followed her briefly before struggling to relocate the two of us.

Butlins holds a special place in the hearts of many Dundonians, even to this day, but it was probably during the 1970s when it enjoyed its peak in popularity and was a fabulous holiday destination. Something which may horrify people today but was totally acceptable back then was the camp offered a babysitting service. To be honest it was hardly what you'd call 'babysitting'. Mums and dads would pay a Butlins employee to stick their heads into the chalets occasionally during the course of the evening and keep a check on their kids while they got pished. My old man and old lady took up this great offer to go and watch Bob Monkhouse who was appearing in the *Pig And Whistle* or *The Beachcomber*. This wouldn't happen in a million years nowadays but it was part of the Great British holiday then and it let the parents get out and get right on the sauce!

6

SANTA'S GROTTO IN A MULTI

For me, Christmas has always been the most special and magical event of the year and I still get excited as an adult each Christmas Eve waiting on Santa's visit. When you were a child the best part was definitely the lead up to the big day and the anticipation and excitement had you hanging off the ceiling.

Certain aspects, however, have changed dramatically over the years and religious folk would argue that the 'true meaning of Christmas' has been lost to outright commercialism and seasonal greed by the retailing industry. Although I wouldn't consider myself religious in any way, they do have a point. The fact is, when you're a child, most of us couldn't give a monkey's if a bairn called Jesus was born in a coo-shed in Bethlehem. We were just glad that three Wise Men had piled in with some gifts and had made a bit of a song and dance about it all and in doing so created the tradition of giving.

I'm sure Mary and Joseph must have been over the moon with the gold but would've probably preferred to ditch the frankincense and myrrh for a cheeky wee bottle of Hai Karate and Chanel No. 5. The two cheapskates who weighed in with those gifts set the standard for generations to come and sent out a totally negative message – that it was ok to hand out shite gifts, even to the Son of God! It's pretty obvious to see that two

37

of the Wise brigade had panic-bought late on Christmas Eve from a branch of Poundstretcher in Nazareth. Millions of people from around the globe have since suffered because of this lack of invention in the present-hunting department and have received keech like socks, outrageously patterned jumpers and compendiums of games.

The great thing back then was Christmas fever didn't really begin until around the second week in December. That's in stark contrast to nowadays when the supermarkets start filling their shelves with mince pies, advent calendars and selection boxes in early September! What the hell is that all about? The food's bound to be fusty before Santa gets anywhere near making a delivery. Children's heads must be turned upside down wondering what's going on, and all of this before we've even got past Halloween!

And while I'm on *that* subject, the bloody Yanks have mugged us and hijacked that festival. When we were young we went out guising around the houses in the scheme. Now, your door gets chapped four or five days before the 31st and the first thing you hear is 'Trick or Treat' from a bairn with a demanding hand out and no sign of wearing any costume. *We* had to work for our dough singing songs and telling jokes. You certainly weren't getting paid for sticking your hand out – you would have got your arse volleyed for cheek. I remember one occasion when my mate Sean and I did a full cabaret performance for a lady in a tenement in Grampian Gardens in Fintry. She sat quite the thing on her settee while we went through all the crap jokes we could remember off of the lollypop sticks. We even bunged in a few songs that we'd actually listened to during some boring school music lessons and at the finish of our show we were sure we'd be a couple of scheme millionaires having given such a long, polished and word-perfect performance. We accepted our payment with extremely good manners and didn't speak to each other till we were well out of her closie.

Sean broke the silence. 'A BLOODY AIPPUHL, AN AIP-PUHL? AN THREE BLOODY PAN-DROPS? Ehv a gade mind tih PAN ir windee in!'

'It coulda been worse. The aippuhls coulda been aff!' Both of us burst out laughing, chomped into our fruit then carried on with the door chapping and guising.

When it came to outfits, creativity and imagination was the order of the day and the challenge was to make something out of nothing. We certainly didn't have ten or fifteen quid to go squandering on a fancy manufactured outfit from a shop.

My last Halloween rant is the touchy subject of lanterns. If one of your mates had turned up to go guising with a pumpkin lantern you would have thought their mum and dad had won the Pools. None of us had ever seen a 'real life' pumpkin. To us it was just a word that sounded like it should be part of the 'flatulence family' such as fart or ripper. 'Hey Jimmy, dih you ken wut a pumpkin is?'

'Eh . . . ehm no sure. Is it a fart thit a bairn wid dae? A sort o mini fart?'

'Eh, that sounds aboot right.'

Our lantern of choice was a dirty big neep knocked out of the nearest farmer's field and laboriously carved out so you could stick your candle in. The results from the finished article left a kind of neep carnage on the ground with enough turnip chips to make a barrel of soup for the whole scheme, not to mention a few near misses with the knife when you nearly sliced your hand open.

Anyway, back to Christmas and as a child I always remember when the old case full of decorations and the tree were taken out of the cupboard and it was time to start getting excited. The decorations that were in the case were a throwback to the Victorian times and must have been handed down through generations of skint Robertsons. Luckily for us my old man was a dab hand with the creativity and set about brightening up our display with some ingenious home-maders. A couple of Fairy Liquid bottles were soon transformed into a brace of Santa's that Tony Hart would have been proud of. This of course was only made possible due to the mysterious 'crepe paper mountain' that appeared from nowhere in the '70s and found its way into everyone's houses. Living rooms were turned into crepe paper shrines as everyone went nuts and paid homage to the Goddess of Crepe Topia.

Most popular by far were the multi-coloured paper chain variety that looked like snowflakes. Rows and rows of them would be pinned or Sellotaped to the roof and would all meet at the light in the middle of the room. Looking at the roof was like looking through a crepe kaleidoscope. Other popular crepe additions were bells that opened like pop-ups, holly, snowmen and Santas. The folk who worked in 'Crepesville' certainly earned their dough and must have been working flat out to keep up with seasonal demand. Sadly, crepe mania died out around the end of the '70s and living rooms went back to being drab and featureless. This was probably due to the fact that the stuff was as flammable as hell and probably responsible for burning loads of people's houses down.

Cotton wool was another material widely used and would turn a dull sideboard into a bonnie wee winter's scene complete with snowmen. It was also used extensively for 'Santa beards'. Our Christmas tree was more of a sapling than a tree, a sorry-looking wee silver number that seemed very sad and lacked self-esteem. In contrast to the present day's all singing, all dancing, colour changing poser range, our little tree was like a withered dandelion that had been pished on by a cat. Still, we did our best and had it decked out in tinsel and baubles and looking as best as it could.

Every year though, without fail, the inevitable happened and the fairy lights didn't work. Sweary words filled the air as the old man painstakingly went round all the little bulbs trying desperately to find the culprit but, once sorted, the homemade star or fairy was placed on the top and the excitement began to rise a few more notches.

Something I failed to highlight earlier that was an essential part of the Yuletide season was the advent calendar. This was usually a bonnie wee Christmassy setting featuring Santa, Rudolf and all the gang and if you were really lucky, it was decorated in glitter. From the first morning in December the big countdown was on and the excitement grew as you opened that first door to reveal a basic picture of a trumpet or a snowflake or a train and the last one was always a double door with Jesus lying glowing angel-like in his manger like a wee Ready Brek extra. If you gave a bairn a calendar like that nowadays they'd chuck it back in yir pus! When *they* open that little cardboard door it bloody well better have chocolate behind it or you're in for a monumental screaming match. And if that's not enough, some even include extra rations up to New Years' Day as well now. Others don't seem to give a damn that it's Christmas and anything goes from Bob the Builder to some crap boy band, each without the slightest hint of the big fat lad from Lapland or a even a wee bell that jingles!

And while I'm on *that* subject, back then Santa was accepted as being a big, overweight, roly-poly galoot who enjoyed the odd pie or two and a dozen pints of heavy. Nowadays the politically correct do-gooders are looking to make him

PC-friendly and chop about nine stones off him! Somehow the thought of Santa with a six-pack, rock hard pectorals and no high blood pressure cheeks is just going too far and messing completely with tradition. He's been a big fat bloke from the days of the cavemen. The vast majority of us don't want him taking out a membership for the Lapland Sports Centre or joining Weight Watchers. His world famous, internationally recognised outfit will not fit him fir a start! Leave him alone!

Christmas 1971 was my first real memory of what it was all about and being aware that when you went to bed on Christmas Eve, and if, as your mum and dad said, 'yid been a good wee boy ah year', then Santa would maybe, just maybe, pay us a visit. Well I must have been a good boy (Santa surely got me mixed up with some other wee laddie!) because next morning he'd left two piles of presents for me and my sister. I clearly recall going into the living room and the first thing I did was look closely at the carpet to see if Santa had left any wet footprints from the snow off his boots. What an arse I was. It wasn't even snowing outside.

I soon forgot about that and set about playing with the cracking wigwam and Indian outfit I'd received. I also got a little electric race track as well which had Matchbox cars going round it. The thing that really sticks in my mind though was a daft wee brown plastic trumpet that Santa had kindly left. However, after about two hours of hammering out some classic contemporary jazz the thing went mysteriously quiet and would only play tunes in the key of 'mute'. For some strange reason it was only blowing out hot air! I now realise what must've happened because I've done it myself as an adult when the need for decommissioning a toy that was 'doin yir napper in' became overwhelming. 'Ach thatz a bummer, the tooter seems tih huv fell oot an itz lost now. Nivir mind, mon wull hae a wee battle wi' yir soajeez.'

During the following couple of Christmas's you were obviously that little bit older, a bit more inquisitive and a whole lot more excitable as Christmas approached. The million-dollar question was inevitably asked, that same one which every parent gets confronted with at some point and must be answered with the utmost guile, cunning, slight artistic license and with a certain degree of fibbing lobbed in for good measure.

'Mummy, how diz Santa git in here? Wir nine flairs up in a multi?'

'Well . . . as yih ken son, Santa's magic an ee yaiziz ah different wehz tih git inti hoosiz,' replied mum contently, patting my head.

'Aw,' I said, none the wiser.

Like I mentioned earlier, my dad's growing skills at self-taught DIY were producing some fine results which pleased my mum no end. The main benefit of this was we had furniture we couldn't normally have afforded plus we didn't have to pay someone to do skilled jobs around the house. To digress from Christmas for a moment, he built a huge wall unit that I must have mistaken for a new climbing frame. Needless to say, after getting near to the top on my maiden expedition, the whole thing detached itself from the wall and came crashing down on top of me, smashing a good few ornaments (that my mum had probably won at the Gussie Park carnival) in the process. Subsequently I got my erse skelped but that didn't stop me having another go at reaching the summit. *CRASH*! Down it came again; cue another tanking from my old man. I got the message that time and my mountaineering career was temporarily suspended.

On the main wall in the living room he'd built an architectural masterpiece – a fireplace complete with 'burning' fibreglass logs. This burning effect was gained via one red light bulb positioned under the logs with a spinning metallic propeller above it. The chimney was a classy affair covered in a fake leather material and decorated with hundreds of studs to give it that medieval look. A striking ornamental coat of arms from Jimmy Reid's shop sat proudly in the centre of it. The living room door didn't escape and was plastered in the same leatherette (rank vinyl) and stud overkill as well. The old man affectionately called this his 'Tudor period'.

Now, everyone knows Santa's preferred method of entry is down your chimney and although we stayed in a multi storey, we thankfully *had* a chimney so the big man should have had no problems in gaining access to our house. The wee wheelies were going round in my head though, trying desperately hard to work out how a fairly portly bloke weighing in at around twenty-eight stones was going to squeeze his gigantic arse through a two-inch gap where the chimney tapered up to the roof. On top of that there were six more storeys above us that he would have to negotiate before he got to ours. Hopefully he would leave his cumbersome sledge, Rudolf, and the rest of the herd up on the multi roof because there's no way my mum would have been happy waking up on Christmas morning with reindeer shite trailed all through her living room! I thought about it, thought about it again then stuck my head up the chimney and had a wee look. 'Ee must be magic right enough,' I half convinced myself, but still, I asked my mum to confirm her theory, just for some reassurance.

She paused then calmly told me, 'If ee struggled wi' the chimney ee wid simply come in through the windee.' If mum says it then it must be true and with that information, Santa must have mastered the technique of abseiling on the Whit-field multis way before the SAS used it to similar effect on the Iranian Embassy. Retrospectively, Santa must surely have had and still have, the biggest reservoir of knowledge on the planet for screwing houses. Whether its tenements, houses, mansions, multis, bolted doors with double mortise locks, highly sophis-ticated security systems, laser beam alarms, CCTV or man-eating Rottweiler dogs, he's never failed in his attempts to gain entry into an establishment and carry out his work. Even more amazing is the fact he's never been caught fae the polis. Not bad for a rather tubby 2,000-year-old man who wears a very distinct bright red suit, has a unique mode of transport and six reindeer (one with a big red nose) as accomplices. In his defence the authorities must turn a blind eye as there's never any damage and he is actually *leaving* something of worth behind (even if it is just a pair of socks or a Teasmade), as opposed to some of the lesser sort of characters of the com-munity who would steal all your worldly possessions *and* your grannie then leave something unpleasant in your chest of drawers!

Another point worth mentioning is, come the time of his final delivery, he must be absolutely blootered! As far back as I can remember me and my sister always carried out the ritual of making sure Santa and Rudolf were well catered for. The old man would go and get out the bottle of cheap, crap whisky which sat at the back of the press (and was probably only drunk by Santa each Christmas Eve) then pour a most generous measure into a glass. We placed this at the fireplace for him to drink at his leisure during the anticipated delivery. A healthy nip in most scheme households must've had him slurring 'Jingle Bells' while trying to drive the sledge straight. Rudolf would get a carrot or half an apple left next to the whisky.

The final piece of the jigsaw was the all-important list. This was the information hotline which let Santa know exactly what you wanted from him. In a somewhat illegible grouping of letters, words were attempted to correspond with the toys on the pages of the Marshall Ward 'Clubbie Book' which my old lady ran. It was simple, you started on the pages where the bikes and 'big expensive' toys were then worked your way through the whole of the boy's toys section and ordered the lot! The one word I did learn to write early was 'and' as this followed every item. By the end, the list filled a roll of wall-paper and was ended with a grateful 'Thank You Santa'. You could just imagine Santa, with a good few whiskies down his gullet and nearing the end of a gruelling shift, coming across a list such as this, 'Here Rudolf, check oot *this* greedy wee bastird!'

'Aw, eez no waantin much eh?'

'Thatz ah wih need at this time o the moarnin! Mih sack's aboot empty an wiv stull got Ormiston an Tranent tih dae. Shove it, wull gie uhm the drum kit. That'll teach eez mum an dad tih lit uhm write an epic like that. Ehl 'Thank You Santa' yih wee gadgie yih!'

(There are no records saying whether or not Santa and Rudolf actually speak with a Dundee accent but you get the idea.)

Seriously though, Steff and me were two of the luckiest kids in the world as our parents must have sacrificed a hell of a lot just to make sure we had a magical Christmas. My dad 'helped' Santa immensely with his intuitive creations; he was like a real life Geppetto which gave us Christmas mornings beyond our wildest dreams. My sister got a shop one year complete with her name on it which had a counter and moved around on castors to serve everyone in the house. I received a magnificent castle built to withstand almost any attack. It had a working drawbridge and portcullis, a huge dungeon and was filled with knights and Crusaders. For the assaulting knights, there were little catapults and a siege tower which rolled up to the walls and allowed the attackers to infiltrate the castle. It was just incredible and I played with that toy until I left my parents' house when I was twenty-four!

Just off our loabee sat what was once a large cupboard. This was converted into what my old man affectionately called 'The Buckie'. I must point out straight away that this was in no way connected to the popular rocket fuel which loads of young Glaswegians regularly scoop by the bucket load. No, this was the workshop where John the Juteworker became Geppetto the Toymaker and Dave the DIY man and created works of art from lumps of wood, pieces of plastic and bits of string. He used to take me into Brian Sheriff's model shop in King Street or The Toy Shop at the bottom of Whitehall Crescent and buy regiments of toy soldiers then we'd go back to The Buckie and he'd meticulously paint their uniforms (even the one-inch miniatures) with unbelievable detail. Sometimes he'd let me be apprentice Geppetto and give me a platoon of Japanese infantry to paint. SPLAT! Ten seconds later they were done, head-to-toe in matt blue. 'Thatz me feenished dad, geez they German paratroopers ower an ehl crack on wi' them?'

'Son here's twa-bob, awa doon tih the shops an git you an yir sister some daintys an choonee. Tak yir time, thirz nae rush tih git back.'

'Aw thanks dad.' It was a kind way of saying, 'Bugger off an awa an play wi' the buses an *EHL* dae the pehntin!'

I remember one time when he'd painstakingly built an Airfix Spitfire model airplane. The camouflage paint had just dried when he proudly presented it to me but then had to watch in horror as I lobbed it across the living room to see if it would fly. Two Cuffs flashed off the back of my nut before ground staff attended the burnt-out wreckage and the plane was taken back into the hangar for repairs.

The Buckie was the scene of a near pre-Christmas disaster when my auntie Alice was up visiting and decided to get up to some mischief. Being only four years older than me she was more like a pal than an auntie and me and Steff followed her about like little sheep. For obvious reasons The Buckie was a no-go zone on the lead-up to Christmas and the door was kept firmly closed by two bolts, one of which was away up in the sky out of us bairns' reach. Enter the cunning auntie Alice who pulled up a stool, undid the bolts and opened the door to paradise. Geppetto's latest work-in-progress was unveiled – a brilliant 4ft x 4ft Wild West scene on a folding board (although I didn't realise that's what it was going to be at the time). Right on cue, Geppetto appeared and went off his rocker, at the same time hurriedly closing the door. Alice got the bollocking from hell and the only reason she escaped a good Wahlupin was down to her being a relative. If she had been a big sister she would have got half-mallied! The funny thing about it was when I burst into the living room on the Christmas morning and saw all these cowboys and Indians shooting it out by the saloon, it didn't even register that this was the same toy. How could it be? The thought was absurd because Santa had brought *this* one!

7

NEW YEAR PEHRTIES
AN ITHER PEHRTIES

Once the initial euphoria of Christmas had died down and the worries of paying back the accumulated debt had been temporarily overlooked, the next big do on the calendar was Hogmanay and celebrating bringing in the New Year. Nowhere else in the world was there a country which celebrated this occasion with such passion quite like the Scots did. The fact that lashings of bevvy went hand-in-hand with this event was possibly the reason why it was so huge in this country. I say 'was' because it's not like that nowadays. Evidence suggests that many Scots have a 'New Year' every week and drink to excess. Social culture has changed so much in the last thirty to forty years – whether it's down to people having more money or cheaper alcohol or just a general shift in attitudes, who knows? True there are those who still celebrate and carry on the old traditions, but arguably and sadly, they are in the minority now. For the generation I grew up with and those who'd gone before, the hoose pehrty and in particular the New Year pehrty was a hugely anticipated event.

Mind you, it wasn't always viewed like that when you were really young. I recall those early parties in the multis vividly and how the initial excitement of having relatives and family friends up quickly gave way to a load of pish-heads gibbering nonsense and staggering all over the shop. On the positive side, when you were wee, people would make a big fuss over you and sometimes hand you a few pennies 'fir yir banky' which was great. You also got to stay up way later than normal. The novelty soon wore off though when the drink kicked in and the conversation altered from one of sensible interaction to sheer and utter codswallop.

Hogmanay itself was commonly a long day as after the word had gone out that 'the Roabeez ir haein a pehrty', you had to wait till the clock struck midnight before your door chapped with the year's 'Furst Fut'. This was a nightmare period in the proceedings, especially if a large mob o weemin had entered.

'Aw Happy New Year mih wee lamb. Geeza big kiss an a cuddle!' That was you done for, there was no escape. Your face was covered with scarlet lipstick then buried in between a massive pair of knockers which were reeking of 'Midnight At The Cowp' – the new fragrance by Guff! In that situation what you really wanted to do was shout, 'Wull yih git the hell aff is Mrs?' but the asphyxiating powers of the two humongous mammaries dictated otherwise. It was a horrendous experience but with the passing of time it was something that you grew to quite enjoy.

At these parties mum's entire Tupperware range was utilised to its full working capacity in an environment it was made for. A Party Susan dish the size of a bin lid was the showpiece of the whole spread and was filled with the usual mix of Spam cubes, pickles, cheese cubes, and pineapple chunks. Why the hell pineapple chunks were always included I'll never know. A stack of cocktail sticks sat in their own little compartment in the middle and the idea was to skewer as many of the chunks as you could and make a kind of mini 'tinky kebab'. The pieces (sandwiches) had a selection of cheese, meat paste and boiled egg on them and were cut into four so it looked like you'd made loads for your guests. If your mum and dad were flush they'd maybe add some Branston Pickle onto the cheese making them pure posh.

A few hours into the party though and these pieces were barely edible due to the acrid fag smoke engulfing them but this didn't deter the revellers. The crisps selection was of the standard variety – plain, cheese and onion, salt and vinegar, etc. Except that is for Twiglets! Whoever decided that branches off a tree dipped in tar then salted would delight the palate of partygoers must have concocted the recipe whilst indulging in an orgy of mind-bending drugs! They were awful and yet they made their way into everyone's party spread. Shoartie (short-bread) was ever present as was Dundee Cake or fruit loaf. It's funny but these two items were only ever consumed at New Year, certainly in our house anyway. These were the days of course when nearly every shop was shut for the holiday period and you had to make sure you had your supplies in.

On the refreshment front it was traditional for the ones hosting the party to supply a large stock of bevvy but occasionally a few of the men would chip in for a couple of kegs of beer which had to be delivered. If the lift was knackered (which it was from time to time) the draymen would have a world-record carry up nine flights of stairs on their hands! Each one held eighty-eight pints and would usually be Pale Ale or Export, a light beer and a darker one. Although widely available, the days of lager dominating the taste buds was still some way off. The beer tins were made of heavy tin and required a little tool which punctured two holes in the top to allow a flow when pouring.

Metal beer tankards were popular back then as were whisky

decanters, all dead posh and real JR's crystal. (I'm sure ours was Tupperware!). Bottles of spirits ranging from OVD dark rum, vodka, whisky, Bacardi and gin sat alongside bottles of Cinzano Bianco, QC sherry and Babycham. Obviously this haul would have cost a fortune to buy so people would usually bring a bottle or half bottle of their favourite tipple. The classic move by some of the more devious party attendees was to bring say a bottle of Nigerian Hyena's Pish Gin, place it in the kitty but drink the 'good' Gordon's Gin. This kind of behaviour was highly frowned upon and could possibly result in the offender being shown the door early for being a 'chancin bastird!'

The record player started off with light 'background' music until the drink set in. The volume was cranked up to 'max' and the space on the living room floor was filled by a mass of inebriation all chanting along to 'Chirpy Chirpy Cheep Cheep'.

'Last night ah heard ma Mamma singin a sa-a-ang, oooh-ee, Chirpy Chirpy Cheep Che . . . Aw Christ, uhv jist stood on the bairn's toy!' A little plastic German Panzer tank versus twelve stones of weight inside a Cuban heel – there could be only one winner.

'Aw uhm sorry son, here's twa pound, git yirsel a new ane. Right, wahr wir wih? Oh eh . . . *Where's yir Mamma gone? Oh where's yir Mamma gone?'*

That was it, it was time to depart and hit the scratcher, inconsolably crying your eyes out at the loss of your tank and all its crew. However, once your head was on the pillow there was no danger you were getting to sleep as the whole house battered out the chorus of 'Lily The Pink' and it wasn't long before some folk 'quietly' staggered into the room to see if you were ok.

NEW YEAR PEHRTIES AN ITHER PEHRTIES

'Well eh wid be o-bloody-k if yih stopped crashin throo mih door an askin if eh wiz sleepin yit!'

Eventually the thumping music went off and you thought, 'At last, time tih sleep, the pehrty's ower.' Oh how *wrong* you were!

'Right c'mon, wahz gonna start the sing-sang aff?' On hearing that cry you lay there looking at the ceiling saying, 'Please God, please tell is eh wiz hearin things there an itz ah a bad dream!'

From through the walls though, the master of ceremonies announces, 'Sssshhh, c'mon now best o order fir Rab. Eez gonna kick aff proceedin's wi' 'The Wonder Of You' beh the King eezsel, Elvis Presley.'

Rab would compose himself then begin but there was always a couple in the corner of the room oblivious to the fact that the records had gone off and the sing-song had started, as they indulged in some drivel about the meaning of life. This blatant act of ignorance was seen as hugely disrespectful to the singer who was trying his best and they'd be nudged and told politely to 'shut thir pusses' while the singer was doing a turn.

Another big no-no was when someone joined in uninvited and sang along with the performer. The MC would call out, 'One singer, one song!' meaning 'rap up and be quiet' as you'll get your turn soon enough. Quiet comments of 'aw, good number' were acceptable, even if it was a song they'd heard the performer sing at a million parties before. Also acceptable was a whole company 'joinee in' on the choruses. This crescendo of bawling didn't go down well at all with any neighbours who had gone to bed early. A broom handle would thump up from the house below or a slipper would stamp down on the roof above. This was usually followed with a roar of, 'WULL YIH SHUT THE FUCK UP!' No-one ever took any notice of these protestations and the party would rage on.

At some point, Steff and me would eventually crash out from sheer exhaustion then some hours later the party would say goodbye to its last reveller. Being young, it was no surprise that we would get up first and start having a carry on and making a racket.

'Wull you twa keep the bliddee noise doon through there! Me an yir mum irna feelin too well!' We'd head up the loabee, open the living room door and set eyes on a scene of total carnage. A Hells Angels stag night would have done well to make this amount of mess! Everywhere you looked there were half full glasses and pint tumblers and the floor was damp or sticky with spilt drink! The stench of stale drink was over-powering. Sideboards, tables and units had cigarette burns on them from people putting their lit fags down for a 'second' then got involved in some conversation and forgot all about them. You can just imagine the same scenario these days where the host had spent a grand on a fancy table from Gillies' shop in the Ferry and someone burnt it with a fag – there would be a riot! Incidents such as these were just part and parcel of having a party.

Some time after my parents had moved into the multis they managed to save a few quid and buy some carpet tiles for the living room. They were like brown nylon *Brillo Pads* and looked awful. They didn't have enough dough to cover the whole floor so my old man painted the exposed floorboards to look like they *were* carpeted. Nobody could tell the difference . . . allegedly! The tiles had hardly had time to settle when they were christened with their first party and were duly burnt with a fag, which went down ever so well with the old lady!

On the odd occasion, a relative or relatives would travel up for a party, usually from down south and be put up for the duration of their stay. This was an arrangement that worked well for both parties as the favour would be returned when needed. One year we had relatives up from England who decided they'd have an extended break and stayed for a week. As was customary, the hosting family would give up their beds and make sure the visitors were made as comfortable as possible. This didn't include extras such as serving them hand and foot and definitely didn't include having the pish ripped out of you. When others are living in your space no matter how well you get on with them, it tests the patience to the limit. There was no effort to muck in and help out and by the end of the week my mum and dad were getting close to giving them a 'high birdy fly' from the ninth floor window. Worse still, when they did finally leave, my mum and dad discovered that their bed had been bizarrely readjusted. All the legs had been unscrewed which was fair enough, but my Matchbox racing track (which was a rather bulky affair and still in its box!), was left underneath creating a weird kind of swivelling surface. Whether it was part of some strange shagging ritual my folks never found out but I was just glad that my beloved toy had survived such a frightening ordeal!

I did have a right giggle one night when I sneaked into my room and placed a plastic crocodile on my sleeping cousin's pillow. Half way through the night all hell let loose when she awoke to find her new 'friend' and screamed the house down. The culprit was never caught!

Sometimes we'd go over to our relatives' house in Kirkton for a party. I enjoyed these dos immensely but the only problem was the getting there and getting back. We didn't have transport or any dough for taxis so it was the long trek from Whitfield through Fintry then along the old Claverhouse

Road. When you're small this was like a Foreign Legion route march over the Sahara Desert. My sister cared not a jot as she was wrapped in ten blankets and strapped into a pram. At night, the old road (a large part of which still exists) was a frightening experience to walk along as the black water of 'The Burnie' (Dichty Burn) flowed menacingly by. I used to think I was going to fall through the fence and roll down the steep embankment and drown in the icy cold water so I'd grip my mum or dad's hand extra tightly for safety.

My dad's sister (Auntie Margaret) and Uncle Andy were two of the kindest people you could meet and with six children of their own, had a lot less than we did financially, but me and Steff were always spoiled over there. Kirkton, like a few other schemes, had a bad reputation at the time, a real rough and tough neighbourhood where it was important to be able to look after yourself. For some folk, especially those with bigger families, it was a daily struggle just to put food on the table. It's no exaggeration that people had to survive on their wits with a combination of tenacious determination and instinct. They also had humour in adversity. Theirs is a separate story altogether which would both shock and amuse with tales of harrowing pain, misery and hardship mixed with warmth and love and some of the best laughs you could imagine.

My cousins' house was massive compared to ours. For a start it was a *proper* house situated at the eastern end of the scheme and had five bedrooms. My cousin Brian laughed when he recalled the years he spent there and said, 'Wih didna hae bugger all tih put on the table fir Christmas denner, nivir mind presents but the New Year pehrties wir mental wi' loads o bevvy!'

Uncle Andy worked for Scottish and Newcastle Breweries and would save up his drink allowance so that Hogmanay and the New Year were celebrated in style. The first day he started there he went into the canteen at the depot, which was up on Old Glamis Road, and grabbed a coffee from the machine before sitting down at a table. Shortly afterwards two workers came in and instantly one of them began sniffing the air then turned to his mate and said, 'Wutz that God awful smell? Itz like coffee!'

Poor Andy sat there with the innocence of 'new guy' syndrome and looked about, wondering what all the fuss was for. The two men spotted Andy's cup and approached him. 'Wut the hell ir yih drinkin *THAT* pish fir?' Andy could only watch, totally speechless as one of the guys picked up the cup and poured the contents down the sink. He produced a tin of beer, pierced the top with the two holes and thrust it into Andy's hand, 'That's wut wih drink in here! Jesus, dinna lit anybody see yih drinkin coffee, yull git slagged tih daith!'

Andy admitted that was the beginning of a long association with the demon drink. As a forklift driver there were numerous occasions when he'd had a wee swally before getting behind the wheel. Many of the metal support pillars in the warehouse were left slightly bent and eventually had to have protective barriers built around them for obvious reasons. One morning though, he topped any of his previous 'bumps' when he forgot to lower his forks and took out a row of valves on the sprinkler system!

The Kirkton parties were always lively affairs with the familiar mixture of dancing, sing-songs and storytelling banter. After a good few bevvies my mum would be up there shakin ir erse and giving it big licks to the records. Unfortunately, her over exuberant dance moves sometimes saw her going over on her ankles and spraining them. Back up she'd get and carry on with the jigging, the pain numbed temporarily by the drink. It wasn't until it was time for the long march back to Whitfield with an ankle or ankles swollen like balloons that she thought that maybe it wasn't such a good idea leaping about like a loony to Slade's 'Mama Weer All Crazee Now'!

It wasn't uncommon back then to have a gatecrasher or two enter into these parties. The old spirit of keeping your door open for anyone and everyone who had a carry-out and wished to join in the festivities was very much alive. The problem with this practice was you just didn't know the person's character. They could be an escaped axe murderer or worse still, not be able to hold their drink. One such character was accepted into the Kirkton congregation one year, although thankfully he wasn't an axe murderer or one who couldn't hold his drink. The problem was he was holding *too much* drink! The guy was on a one-man mission to drink the house dry and relieve it of any alcohol content and when he started going through to the kitchen and helping himself, drastic measures had to be taken. To make matters worse, he was boasting about how much he could handle. In short, he was a complete arse.

At house parties one of the perks when you were younger was being asked to do the bar. This saved the adults from interrupting their busy drinking, dancing and singing schedules and more often than not, you were financially rewarded for your efforts. It was your duty to make sure no-one's glass went to empty which was quite a challenge during the periods of heavy and sustained swallying. Taking cans through for the men was the easy part of the job and occasionally you'd give it a right good shake in the kitchen before handing it to them then watch from afar as it exploded all over the place. Too many of these though and you could expect to be suspended from your post as bartender. Pouring nips and getting the measure correct was a bit trickier and these usually ended up as triples or quadruples. When the adults winced and their faces screwed up after taking a sip you knew you'd went too far but in saying that, they rarely handed them back for diluting.

The gatecrasher had begun bypassing my cousins' bar services and was pouring himself very generous nips from the first bottle he came to. Brian didn't hold back and challenged him, 'Hey pal, calm doon a but, yir gonna feenish ah the drink.'

'Eh brought a half bottle in,' he protested.

'Eh but yih feenished that aboot *twa oors ago!*' Amongst family and friends, drinking way more than your quota wasn't an issue in the slightest but for a stranger, this was bordering on taking the extreme pish. When he'd gone back through to the living room Brian said, 'Right, wull soart this boy oot nae problem.' They began putting some 'additional mixers' into his drink like *Vim* scouring powder, washing up liquid and various other kitchen products. For a while they had no effect and the gatecrasher kept knocking them back and bragging until he began quite literally foaming at the mouth and blowing bubbles. The 'bar staff' thought this was hilarious but after he'd been shown the door and sent on his way, Auntie Margaret stormed into the kitchen shouting, 'Yiz coulda bliddee killed him yih stupid buggers!' but she saw the funny side of it afterwards.

There was an instance at one party where if it hadn't been for the help of a few revellers, a passing drunk in the street may have passed away completely. He wasn't so much a gate-crasher, more of a 'hedge-crasher'. On what was a bitterly cold night a chance glimpse out of a window alerted the rest of the party that someone looked like they were in trouble. My cousin Brian and a couple of others went out to see what the problem was. They found a man utterly inebriated and motionless, who was slumped over their fence and half buried in the hedge.

'Itz a but caald fir burd-nestin.'

'Eez mibbee spotted a *penguin's* nest!'

'A penguin couldna survehv in these temeperatures, itz absolutely baltic!' Every surface in the street was white, covered with a thick frost and the guy was freezing to touch. Luckily, they managed to wake him from what would have been a certain deathly slumber and revived him as best they could before he slurred and assured them he'd be fine to stagger home. What he didn't realise was that he'd just 'paid' one of his rescuers for the privilege of saving him from hypothermia. One of the rescue team was a member of the notorious Kir'tin Huns gang and wasn't slow to seize an opportunity, especially if it was of the earning variety. While the others were rubbing the guy and trying to put some heat back into his body, one pair of hands was removing a wallet and cash from his pockets. True, the guy *was* still alive, albeit a wee bit 'lighter' than he was prior to his hedge kipping escapade!

As a bairn, the return marches from the Kirkton parties, sometimes at four or five in the morning, were truly horrendous affairs. Admittedly, it was this kind of character-building torture which made the nation great – 'Jist git on wi' it. Yir tired? Keep marchin an shut yir girnin pus! Itz bla'in a blizzard? Pit yir hood up an keep marchin, wir jist aboot there.' We were nowhere near 'jist aboot there' but you kept marching and complaining through the tears and eventually developed a stiff upper lip, or more accurately, a 'numb' upper lip . . . and ears . . . and nose . . .

NEW YEAR PEHRTIES AN ITHER PEHRTIES

As the hour was late, me and my sister were usually sleeping under all the coats by the time my parents decided to hit the road so being wrenched from the warmth of a house out into the pishing rain or sleet with a force ten gale in the face was a little uncomfortable. The march was made even more delightful when my mum and dad were having a verbal scrap. One such barney which had been going full tilt from Kirkton ended near Mill o' Mains when my old man announced, 'Thatz it, ehm off, see yih!' and he walked away into the darkness of Caird Park. When you're really young and witness something like that it's devastating. I thought my old man was off for good, the most special man in my life, gone – never to be seen again! It's thoroughly heart-breaking when you're too young to understand that parents sometimes fall out, and mine did in those early years. I toddled home the rest of the way holding onto my wee sister's pram and greetin my eyes oot while my old lady threw curses into the night. The old man? Well, he went to sleep on his mate's settee in Princes Street and returned home next day with a thumper of a hangover to face the music.

There were, of course, very rare times when my parents must have been slightly flush and we travelled home in a taxi. Oh how I savoured those journeys. Better still was when I was allowed to stay with my cousin John, who was a few years older than me. We got on great and he would take me to all the adventure hotspots in Kirkton and the surrounding areas. When you were an outsider in a foreign scheme the local junior Mafia viewed you with some suspicion until they knew you were a guest of a relative, then you were granted temporary diplomatic immunity from getting your head kicked in.

Sometimes my auntie Margaret would let us take some of

the empty lemonade bottles from the previous night's party along to the shops and get the one penny back on each of them. To us, this was the equivalent of a birthday or Christmas present and we'd buy as many sweets as we could.

My mum's mother and father (Nobby and Bett) lived in Fintry in a semi in Findcastle Place and the majority of Hogmanays were spent there. New Year was a huge and special event for them and the planning was of military precision. They'd begin by saving up months in advance and stockpiling crates and crates of beer and also buy a bottle of each of the main spirits. Everyone knew the festivities kicked off there, seeing out the old and bringing in the new. Their living room wasn't that big and was always chock-a-block as was the kitchen, and still the door would go and more bodies would pile in.

My grandparents both smoked as did my mum and all bar one of my aunties and uncles. In fact, it seemed like everyone smoked back then. At first it wasn't too noticeable but as the soiree progressed the top of the room would fill with a thick blanket of poisonous smoke which gradually got thicker and began getting lower and lower. At times it was so dense that you had to look under the level to identify bodies on the other side of the room! You can imagine how the egg pieceys tasted after being subjected to that for a few hours but everyone just got on with it.

My granddad's Black Watch buddy Alex Mac would turn up with his squeezebox and start rattling the tunes out prompting the coffee table to be removed and the dancing to commence. It was like a twenty-four-man 'Strip The Willow' in a phone box as folk went birlin an hoochin an choochin out of control. The central theme of the Findcastle shindigs, much like the parties in the multis, was definitely the sing-song and it was a battle between my gran and granda to see who could hold the floor as both of them were very good chanters.

The very mention of a sing-song had some people's arses fainting and trying to evacuate the room. This was a traditional spinning of an empty bottle in the middle of the floor and whoever the top pointed at they had to perform. Some would shift in their seat to try get out of the line of fire and remonstrate, 'Itz pointin at hur,' or, 'Eh canna sing the now, ehv no hud enough drink.' Resistance was futile and with a room full of characters heckling, you bloody well *were* singing as it was expected.

The confident singers in the room would have a few numbers in their repertoire and belt one out at the drop of a hat. Others like my mum and dad were mainly one-song-wonders. This was a song they'd taken time to learn the words of and through time became 'their' song. It then got to the stage where people would say, 'C'mon John, gie wih "The Wild Rover",' or, 'Margaret, gaun dae "Ten Guitars"?' As the years went by it got to the stage where I'd follow that request and say to myself, 'Aw fir crehin oot loud no "THE WILD ROVER"!' However, I have to admit it does still give me a warm feeling in my heart to hear them.

Any lull during the sing-song and my gran would wade in with a 'filler'. She seemed to know loads of songs and once she started that was it. My granda would maybe squeeze in a sentimental number about losing some mates in the Second World War, the whole room hanging on every word and note and caught up in the emotion of it all then in she'd burst with another. He'd famously call out to her, 'Yir giein meh erse a sair hade!' which basically translated into, 'Fir Christ's sakes wummin, wull yih shut the hell up!'

I don't remember the record player being on much at the

Findcastle parties. My gran and granda much preferred the tradition of homemade entertainment and creating your own fun and another great pastime they had was party games. Sadly, a lot of these games, just like the old songs, have been swallowed up and lost in the jaws of modern culture. Just as the older generations pass away, so too do some of the traditions and the fun that went with them. In most cases nowadays an iPod docking station is switched on for the duration of the soiree and you're subjected to hours of thumping beats. The whole interaction thing seems to have disappeared. Maybe I'm just being nostalgic but seeing a room full of half-pished adults with pink lipstick dots all over their face and trying to remember how many were there, was a right hoot. I can't remember the finer details of the game but each time you got the question wrong you got another dot. The real drunks ended up totally pink!

Another game involved the men and women splitting up with one party going through to the kitchen and each team would conjure up some embarrassing act for a chosen victim from the rival crew. This usually involved a blindfold for the unfortunate soul and one I remember in particular was when one of the men had to go into the ladies' company. They'd have him all wound up and hot under the collar then tell him to stick his lips out thinking he was away to get a big kiss when – *Wahlup!* – he'd get a sour half lemon slapped in his pus!

Best one of all though was a game I'm sure was called 'Forfeits' where you'd be given a task or a dare to carry out. Sometimes players would be sent to a neighbour's house up the street and have to ask for a 'piece on jam' or a 'slice o cheese' or something and if the door chap proved fruitless, they have to keep visiting houses till they got the goods. Occasionally a player would get waylaid at another party and return about an hour later after a couple of nips and a song. It was great fun indeed and most people happily participated in the nonsense.

Having the neighbours in meant there was a real community feel and it was a great way of getting to know them better. My granda had to lob one out though one New Year when they'd come in blootered and kept spilling their drink all over the carpet. Spillages were part and parcel of having a shindig but Nobby had a very low toleration for folk who couldn't handle their drink, especially ones who constantly kicked it all over the floor.

'Right thatz the last ane, yiv got the place bliddee sailin. Yid be better lehin on the flair, thirz mair drink doon there than wutz goin in yir mooth!' and without waiting for a reply he grabbed him by the scruff of the neck and the arse of his trousers and launched him out the front door. As an ex-bouncer at The Tonk (The Empress) and other noteworthy establishments, this came as second nature but as it was the New Year he refrained from following up with part two of the ejection and left the neighbour's jaw intact!

Both my uncles (John and Alex) followed my granda's lead and joined the military in different capacities. The former went into the Black Watch Territorial Army while Alex joined the Scots Guards regulars. Alex was among the first soldiers posted to Northern Ireland in the late '60s when tensions were running high between Catholics and Protestants. At first he said the Catholic community welcomed the soldiers' presence on their streets and would offer cups of tea to the men. This friendly relationship changed drastically after a series of events in the early '70s when soldiers shot and killed members of the Catholic community, none more controversial than the 'Bloody Sunday' massacre in January 1972 by the Parachute

Regiment. Throughout this decade in particular, the army suffered casualties as 'The Troubles' escalated and every family who had a son serving worried constantly about receiving news of an injury or death. The death of any service-man who lived in the Dundee housing schemes was greeted with shock and disbelief and being so close to home the effects were devastating. Even as a youngster you were aware of the situation over in Northern Ireland as it featured regularly on the news and I remember my gran's anguish and worry when her son was away on a Tour.

Uncle Alex was a larger than life character who thrived on having a laugh and getting up to mischief, someone who was full of devilment but in a warm and friendly way. This often led to him spending numerous spells behind bars in the Guard House for plesterin aboot! His real focus though was his family, especially his mum and dad and being home for Hogmanay to see in the New Year with them meant every-thing to him. As a serving soldier in Her Majesty's Armed Forces the job often dictated otherwise and he was hardly ever free during that period. That was the official line. The unofficial line involved a wee extension of his army leave otherwise known as AWOL (absent without leave). Because we had no phone my mum would receive a telegram saying he was coming up but don't let on to their mum and dad as he'd surprise them at the Bells. On one occasion he'd been home on official leave but this ended the day before Hogmanay and he was due to go back to Germany where his regiment was stationed. The train got as far as Newcastle when he turned to his soldier buddy who was also travelling back and said, 'Wiv got twa choices here. Wih stye on this train an head back tih Germany wahr wull hae a shite New Year or wih kin git aff now, head back tih Dundee tih wir ane fowk an hae a proper knees-up an a right good pish-up.'

Moments later they were standing on the Newcastle platform searching the timetable for the next available train north. Everyone was overjoyed to see him step over my gran's door as her 'first foot' and all she could do was hug him tightly and say, 'You, yir an affy bugger!' After two weeks of lying low he knew full well he'd be thrown straight in the military jail in Germany on his return. 'But oh how it wiz worth it,' he said.

During another New Year gathering my gran took a break from the festivities and commented how low she was feeling at not having her son there together with the rest of the family. No sooner had she uttered the words than my granda told my dad to 'pit a load o tins in a bag fir a kerry-oot. Wir goin tih git uhm!' He was stationed at Redford Barracks in Edinburgh and couldn't get back to Dundee so they planned to go and get him. Despite scooping plenty of ale before they got into my granda's old Ford Cortina, they never gave it a second thought and screamed off towards 'Auld Reekie'. Although laws had been introduced in the 1960s with regards to drinking and driving, many drivers didn't see anything wrong with bevvying and getting behind the wheel which nowadays seems positively ludicrous. Thankfully, they arrived safely in Edinburgh only to find my uncle had bailed out and was already on his way to Dundee. My old man admitted he was 'shitin eez drahrz' on the return journey as my granda joined in the scooping while planting the accelerator pedal firmly on the deck. Again, and incredibly, they made it back in one piece to find Alex with a tin of beer in his hand holding court in the living room.

As we grew that little bit older the days of having to listen to 'the rabble next door' whilst trying to sleep were soon forgotten and we were able to appreciate the whole culture of the parties. One of my favourite memories from all those times was getting a glass of blackcurrant or red Cordial juice. It must have been fairly expensive because I only ever remember getting it at my gran's during the New Year. It had a very unique and distinct taste and as bairns we classed this as our 'bevvy' and savoured every drop of it, and of course the thicker it was the better. We'd mimic the adults and kid on it was 'goin tih oor hades an wih wir feelin slightly pished!' Eventually, the time would come when you did taste real alcohol and it was a horrible, bitter and unforgettable experience, not like now where some bevvy tastes better than proper soft drinks. Taking a swig of Export or Pale Ale was like licking a window with a seagull's shite on it! Whisky was even worse and the smell alone was enough to put anybody off drinking forever! How I wish I still had that same taste and thought process now!

Although the memories are delightfully rich and happy I'm only grateful that I wasn't of drinking age in the years before the ones I've covered. Like I explained earlier, a huge quantity of drink would be stockpiled for months and the first party would kick off at my gran and granda's house then they'd go on a daily tour around all the various relatives and friends' houses. The festivities only ended a week later when all the spare drink which hadn't been consumed was cached together and brought back to the original venue for one almighty and final knees-up. Now that was a liver-busting New Year celebration on a colossal scale!

8

MOVIN HOOSE

Living in the Whitfield housing scheme in 1974 was comparable to living in war-torn Beirut – only rougher! In the short space of five years or so, it had gone from an architect's dream of a model, modern day estate into a place where even the muggers walked the streets in fear and wild dogs ran around in packs for their own safety. Gangs of youths patrolled the turf and frequently indulged in running battles with rival gangs who were hoping to 'invade' their territory. I am exaggerating ever so slightly but at times it *was* bad.

The visionary Skarne tenement system which was the largest of its kind in Britain and had worked so well in Sweden flopped big time. The one-time pillaging, raping, house-burning Viking mobs of bygone Norse folklore had become mild-mannered, passive, semi-jessies who found neighbourly love and harmony living in the Skarne housing in their native land. However, the same ethos didn't transport very well over the North Sea and the Dundee fowk embraced it as warmly as they would having a breeze block dropped onto their toes. It just wasn't happening, not in a million years! The two cultures weren't just separated by a stretch of water – they were worlds apart! Somehow, you just couldn't imagine our Scandinavian cousins living the same lifestyle.

Banging on the wall, 'Ho Olaf, wull yih turn they effin ABBA records doon afore eh shove that Napoleon an eez Waterloo right up yir arse! Ehm trehin tih enjoy a quiet wee swally an git mih leg ower here! Eh mean it Freda, if eh hae tih go an chap that door once mair, ehl rap him right in the pus!'

'Och c'mon Sven, jist firgit ah the bangin an thumpin. How aboot pourin me anither wee gless o Pomagne?'

In the years which followed, the depravation and social decay escalated at a steady rate and the scheme was to gain the kind of notoriety that certainly no-one living there ever wished for. As I commented earlier, most people and most definitely us bairns, just got on with it. There was just too much fun to be had. My folks decided to move out of our multi hoose in that year of '74, not because of any negative shit that was hitting the Whitfield fan, the sole reason was space. We only had two bedrooms and, thinking ahead, my mum and dad decided to move sooner rather than later and thankfully spared me and my sister the uncomfortable scenario of still sharing a room in our late teens and sleeping in bunk beds!

My mum broke the news very gently to us and said, 'Right you twa, git ah yir toys packed up, wir movin tih Fintry.' Although I was seven years old and could chuck a dockie from the edge of Whitfield into Fintry, for all I knew, this place where we were moving to called 'Fintry' could have been on the south side of Jupiter. Sure we were streetwise and had been let out to play from a very young age, and my gran and granda had a house there, but retaining information like place names or street names wasn't nearly as important as knowing how to start a fire behind the shops or knowing how many Black Jacks you could get for two bob. This was going to be just one big adventure. Yes I was sad to be leaving my mates behind, and when the living room door shut in 9E Whitfield Court I may even have felt a wee pull on the heartstrings at leaving behind the medieval chimney that Santa had squeezed his big fat arse through, and the 'North Face of the Eiger climbing unit' which had beaten me on those two occasions. I entered the lift with my mum and dad and wee sister and watched, for the last time, the numbers drop from 9 to Ground. Then I forgot all about Whitfield and wondered where the hell we were going.

It didn't even register that we'd travelled less than half a mile westwards to reach our new family abode in Fintry Road which, on the outside, looked like it had been by used by Johnny Weissmuller for filming some jungle scenes in *Tarzan*. Both the front and back gardens were seriously overgrown and in need of a good crew cut. The backies were exceptionally messy with many items of furniture lying in the long grass, having obviously been tossed out. The inside fared even worse and had definitely been carpet-bombed by a B-52 bomber. It brought a whole new meaning to the word 'shitehouse'!

Every room was like a tip with more scattered furniture and old newspapers strewn around. The best one of all was the bathroom which had black wallpaper and these shrewdly cut seagulls from some other wallpaper stuck on top. They hadn't bonded to the roof very well and their wings were hanging down limply, giving the impression that they were flying about – or maybe that was the whole idea? The place needed a severe comb with a bulldozer and the clear up operation took a good few weeks but gradually it began to feel like a home to us.

The initial shock of seeing such a hole had been lightened considerably the day before we moved. My dad had won £112 on the Taypools football coupon which was like a squillion quid in today's money. It was a huge amount of dough for my parents to win and it went a hell of a long way to making it a more stress-free move. As well as a load of other small accessories my mum went and treated herself to her very first washing machine, a twin tub which gobbled up the bulk of the money. She couldn't believe that she'd be able to do the washing in her own house from now on and hang it in her own back garden. What didn't change though was the odd bout of snowdropping and she quickly realised that stealing items from your washing line was every bit as popular in one scheme as it was in another.

Moving from what had originally been a brand new flat in Whitfield to a semi-detached, mid-terraced house in Fintry with a history of having been screwed a few times and looked like a dive had 'bad move' written all over it. Although Whitfield was spiralling downwards, the scheme we had just moved to made Whitfield look like Utopia. Built just after the Second World War, Fintry (until the completion of Whitfield) grew to become the largest of all the Dundee housing schemes by far but during the 1960s things had turned pretty sour and with that came a whole load of bad press. Problems with gangs, high unemployment, vandalism and graffiti all contributed in some way to the estate getting a bad name in various quarters. It's fair to say, just like any other scheme, there were undoubtedly problems but many tenants lived perfectly happy existences. The social problems carried into the early 1970s and to add to the mix the practice of 'moonlighting' had reached epic proportions. This was the name given to the action where tenants (who owed the City Factor a large amount of rent money) buggered off, usually at night and basically disappeared off the radar.

The old man set to work straight away with some learn-as-you-go DIY and indulged in both construction and destruction. First to go were the seagulls – they were punted back to the sea cliffs of Arbroath. The old stone fireplace was ripped out also. In the kitchen the old man took one look at the big, deep porcelain sink and said, 'No way!' He 'dropped' a hammer on it which unfortunately left a dirty big crack then went down to the Factor's to complain, 'Eh, itz mih sink, itz nae yase. Itz got a but o a crack in it.'

'That's no problem Mr Robertson; we'll have someone out immediately to see to that.'

The guy was true to his word but the end result wasn't the one the old man was looking for. Unaware, mum broke the news to him when he got in from work, 'John, the boy wiz up the day aboot the sink. Thatz it ah done.' Thoroughly impressed with the speed and efficiency with which this was executed he went to have a look at his 'new' sink. 'Wut the bliddee hell is *that?*' he bawled. 'The boy's jist fuhlled it wi' putty!' Back to the office he went where the guy explained that it was 'only a crack and the putty would do for a good while'.

'Oh wull it?' he thought. He returned a third time and relayed to Mr Factor the 'tragic accident' that had occurred in our kitchen.

'Well, mih wife wiz busy daein the dishes when shih tripped on this hammer an battered irsel aff the weakened sink. It jist split right in half, made a hell o a mess.' Shortly afterwards my mum was doing the dishes in her new top-notch stainless steel sink!

One project which had occupied my dad's mind since the day we moved in was the wall which separated the kitchen and the coal bunker and how best to remove it, which would increase the space in the room. So, when he got wind that the housing officers were in the scheme planning for the massive re-wiring programme, he seized the opportunity with both hands (wrapped around a sledgehammer). With no time to lose, the wall was demolished and heaved out into the back garden then he hastily decorated over the cracks. With impeccable timing an inspector turned up the following day to sort out where the points and wiring routes would go throughout the house. The wallpaper was still wet as the guy entered the kitchen to carry on with his calculations. Something was missing? According to the drawings, the two hundred other houses he'd visited showed a wall with a doorway but for some reason this one was unique. Maybe the builders had been inebriated and simply 'forgot' to add one onto this house? The old man stayed silent but inside he was flapping like hell, 'Fir Christ's sake, dinna look oot that back door!' He was very grateful when the guy made some 'slight readjustments' and carried on with his work!

When he ripped out the old fireplace the old man had progressed to the dizzy heights of 'Master DIY Anorak', and he felt it was only right to mark the occasion with a new feature in the living room – another fireplace and chimney. It was a return to his successful 'Tudor period' which had served him so well in the multis. With the advanced skills he had learnt and the knowledge he had gained, this new and ambitious showpiece addition would take centre stage and instantly endear itself to any visitors. Either that or they could use it in a more practical manner and plant their erses on it for a seat.

He had a couple of problems though. Firstly a lack of materials and then secondly, when he located a supplier, a lack of labourers willing to carry out the work. After building a base wall with coping-stone he roped me into (or rather telt me I would be!) accompanying him on a highly illegitimate venture. He put on his old boiler suit and said, 'C'mon, wir goin awa tih git some stanes.' He'd 'acquired' a large wheelbarrow from his work (along with a bag of cement) and wheeled it all the way to Fintry from the Arbroath Road. Then he broke up the old fireplace, filled the barry with heavy rubble and off we went to the country road which leads to the little village of Duntrune. About halfway up he stopped on the road and said, 'Right, this'll dae wih here. Wull dump the crap then git the stanes.'

As second in command and only a mere young labourer I had no input whatsoever into the planning and building of the fireplace but, given my lowly position in the old man's blossoming DIY company, I still understood that he would need materials to carry out the work. I looked around and couldn't for the life of me see any builder's merchants to supply the necessary stone. 'Right, start takkin they stanes there and lob thum inti the barry an shift yir erse, wih dinna waant tih git nabbed.' My old man's supplier didn't actually know he was a supplier but the stones from his dry-stone dyke fitted the bill for his project.

'Yih canna tak them dad, yull git lifted!'

'Hud yir wheesht an keep graftin or yir pocket money'll be gittin docked!' The barry weighed a ton for the return journey and the old man had to keep stopping for a rest as he was breathin oot eez erse by then. When we finally reached the house and dumped the load I thought, 'Great, we've made it an nae interference fae the fermir or the Fuzz.' The happiness was short-lived though as I was informed we'd have to repeat the process a couple of more times.

And so, with base established, a new school to go to, new friends to meet, new places to explore and new capers to get up to, Fintry was about to show me what it had to offer as a playground.

9

SKALE DAYS

For a great many youngsters, setting off for that first day at school marks a monumental turning point in their lives, a first episode in the old coming of age thing where a certain degree of independence is given and you have to take on the 'big bad world'. For others it is nothing short of a living nightmare when they are plucked from the reassuring embrace of their mummy's arms and left to fend for themselves among the wolves.

As was common with the majority of bairns from the Whitfield housing scheme, I wasn't lucky enough to attend a nursery and had to make do with an apprenticeship served on the streets and the odd bit of advice from mum and dad. The latter consisted of, 'Dinna be gittin inti any baather an smashin windeez,' and, 'Mind an be in fir yir tea!' All other life skills you learned as you went along and these covered a range of subjects:

Sociology – you quickly learned that if you gave a boy who was two years older and two feet bigger than you a bit of lip, you were going to get a rap in the pus!

Geography – At four years old, it was essential that you knew your immediate surroundings so you knew where to have loads of fun and knew how to get home in time thus avoiding a *Cuff*.

P.E. (physical education) – This was also self-taught and honed to perfection. If you were a fat bastard there's no way you could get up onto walls and roofs to play and you were also more likely to get caught from the Fuzz if you were up to no good.

Science – You learned to run like hell when, whilst standing round an 'illegal' bonfire, someone decided to conduct a scientific experiment and lobbed a gas or aerosol canister into the flames to see what would happen!

Arithmetic – This was one of the fundamental skills you learned before you even learned how to kick a ball. If you found a two-bob bit on the street, it was important to know how many sweets you could buy with it. Also, many games required excellent numeric skills like, for instance, hide-and-seek. If you couldn't count to twenty and give people a chance to hide then you were no use to anyone and you'd be told to go and 'play wi' the lassies'.

English – Writing and spelling were practiced with pieces of chalk on walls and paths and gradually you began to make basic words which were often of the sweary genre. Some worthies progressed to the darker side of literacy and began using permanent marker pens and spray cans. Most street students were probably unaware that they were also learning a second language. Speaking 'Oary' (Dundonian) came naturally in the schemes, it was in the blood and genes, but bairns needed to become fluent in the Queen's English as well when in the company of adults who practiced 'pan-loafy' (attempting to talk polite shite!) and who took a dim view of the 'peasant tongue'.

It didn't take too long before you were operating to Degree Level in all of these subjects and more than ready for your first day at school. Extra-curricular subjects such as tying shoelaces and school ties were not all that important and could be picked up at a later date.

The only thing I really remember from my first day at Greenfield Primary School was when our mums left the class to let us get on with it and this laddie started screaming like a wee lassie. Each time his mum went to leave he became even more hysterical and this went on for a good while. He eventually clamped up but by then we all had the earache.

I'm not sure how far the walk was from the multis to the school but it seemed like about twenty miles. You were escorted by your mum for a couple of days and shown the route there and back then that was it – you were on your tod. There was none of this nonsense you get nowadays where bairns are ferried via pre-heated cars right to the school gates (and sometimes through them!) then picked up again at night. The first drop of rain or the slightest of breezes and the ignition keys are turning. For a start, many families didn't have cars but even if they did there's no way you'd be getting pampered with a lift.

'Ach mum, ehm jist gonna hae a lang leh the day. Geeza shout aboot twenty-tih-nine an hae mih Cinnamon Grahams on the table an mih chocolate an crisp-loaded packed lunch riddee.'

SKELP!

I don't know why but I developed a worrying appetite for

throwing stones at a very young age. This may sound innocent enough when the targets are tin cans on a wall but when I tell you that sometimes it was people's heads then it was *extremely* worrying! I'm ashamed to admit that on a few occasions when the final bell went and everyone formed a heaving throng to get out of the main gates and make their way home, I would launch stones indiscriminately into the crowd. The only result of doing something as reckless and stupid as that was injuring little people like me and I recall with utter horror the terrible screams when I split someone's head open. Worse still, I was never caught and punished for it. Yes, I was a total horse's arse but hopefully I've received enough bad karma over the years to pay me back for the pain on those innocent cracked skulls.

It's sad to think that that is the main memory I have of my year and a bit spent at Greenfield. No doubt when I left, my ex-fellow pupils must have noticed a one hundred percent drop in coupons being rattled by random dockies falling from the sky. When we moved to Fintry I was still in Primary 2 and because of where our house was situated it fell into the catchment area for Longhaugh Primary School. For some odd reason I didn't go there which was probably a godsend for the neighbouring school of nearby St Lukes. Some Catholic heads may well have been throbbing after straying into my line of fire during the annual tear-up on St Patrick's Day.

Dundee, thankfully, has never had the same problems with religion that Glasgow and other parts of the West Coast have. But for as long as anyone can remember, every 17th of March pupils from Catholic and Protestant schools had a go at one another. It was Cathies against Proddies and it was ludicrous! In my old man's day it was Scots and Irish day with the same war being waged against people who were mates for the other

364 days of the year. None of us understood it but you joined the pack with a 'mob mentality' and safety in mind. My dad is in fact a Catholic, my mum a Protestant and me and my sister were also christened Protestant. But for all I care I could be a Buddhist astronaut from the Church of Lesser Day Sandal Sniffers and it wouldn't alter how I feel about my family, friends and people in general.

In the end I was enrolled and joined the register of pupils at Fintry Primary School. Since moving home all that had occupied my mind was the worry of going to a new school as a standout 'new boy'. I wasn't a scrapper by any means and I was shitting myself that lads would be queuing up to offer me a square-go at the first playtime and see exactly where I'd fit into in the pecking order. These are the jungle rules and millions of years of evolution have had little impact in altering this fact. When the day's final bell went and I received no knuckle sandwiches I thanked my lucky stars and was grateful for my non-threatening look.

The days turned into weeks and gradually I began to be accepted and make friends within the class. However, you are still under the microscope, being assessed by everyone and you are doing likewise sussing folk out. One boy in the class stood out more than any others as 'one to watch', not for being a bully or anything like that. He was just one of those lads who weren't quite all there in the nut and it showed. One day one of the twin girls in the class put her hand up then informed the teacher that her Mars Bar had gone missing from her bag and assured her that it had been there earlier. The teacher didn't have to indulge in too much detective work as the 'chocolate thief' turned himself in without knowing. He may have been a prime suspect anyway, given the position of his chair and the bag hanging on the back of the seat which was only an arm's length away. But a vital piece of evidence presented itself and the trial was concluded swiftly.

'Barry, did you take Sarah's Mars Bar?' He looked at her with his big brown eyes and said, 'No Miss, it wizna me, honest.'

'I think the chocolate covering your face would suggest otherwise, don't you think?'

'It wizna me Miss.' And he believed himself while the jury of thirty-one didn't.

'Ehl better keep mih eh on him,' I thought.

Fintry must have been one, if not *the* only school where they made the boys wear shorts until the end of Primary 6. And they were *proper* shorts, not like the ones footballers wear nowadays where they can just about tuck them into their socks. This idea worked very well during the hot and balmy summer months but when things turned nasty and Mother Nature gritted her teeth during autumn and winter, it became a battle for survival. The feeling of hailstones thrashing in horizontally against your legs in a Force Ten gale was character building of the highest order. It was like being stung in the legs from a thousand giant hornets. All except the Primary 7 boys went through the winter months with blue legs. Getting a snowball slammed off a hypothermic leg was not funny in the slightest.

Wellies, as I touched on earlier, were the footwear of choice as soon as the first few flakes of snow began to fall. When I say 'choice' it was more a case of being telt fae yir mither and forced to wear them. I don't think our parents were of the generation who had worn wellies or it sure as hell didn't seem that way. Having felt the excruciating numbness of toes inside a wafer-thin rubber coating first hand, there's no way they'd subject their offspring to the same torture. They quite clearly hadn't and mums the length and breadth of the country thought these boots were the 'bee's knees' for both rainy and snowy weather.

Freezing or not, the sight of a virgin blanket of snow covering the scheme on a school morning was like finding a ten-bob bit on the ground – highly exciting! Apart from birthdays, it was probably the only other time when you got up sharp without a second or third bawl from your mum. You knew it was going to be a fun-packed day with loads of snowball target practice and building slides. Once you'd convinced your old lady that wearing wellies was a danger to your health, you'd rake out your special 'slidey' shoes. These were usually an old pair which still fitted but were kept especially for the winter conditions. The ideal shoes for sliding were Wedgers with the soles worn down smooth as marble for a frictionless glide. Two or three of us who were first in in the morning would tramp and flatten the snow then begin sliding over it repeatedly until it became gleaming ice. Pretty soon there'd be about fifteen to twenty kids queuing up to have a go. Everyone would be having a ball until someone turned up and tried to slide down it with inappropriate footwear where the cry would go up, 'Git aff the slide wi' they Springers on, yir ruinin it yih prick!'

Springers were hugely popular shoes in the late 1960s and throughout the '70s and became one of the main choices of footwear for the Northern Soul punters. They were a definite no-no on slides though as the segs (metal protectors) which were hammered into the leather soles ripped up the highly polished surface. It was like someone skating with a pair of crampons on and they were politely 'told' to go and make a snowman or partake in something else. Or they'd maybe be set upon by a mob and given a 'Be-Ro'. This name was taken from the popular brand of flour and an advert on TV at the time where a little cartoon man in a black suit was covered in the white powder. This was re-enacted as a punishment and the victim would be grabbed and chucked onto the deck then everyone would kick loads of snow over them and leave the poor soul looking like the Be-Ro man. I endured a few of these myself and the cold snow got everywhere under your clothes.

If you were really cool you'd take a big runny and perform a crouched down slide which was called a 'wee mannie'. You could also get a wee mannie holding onto the bottom of a mate's duffle coat and getting them to pull you round the playground. It was a bummer though when their foot slipped backwards and you caught a heel in the shin. One of the most frightening things about sliding was when it was maybe only a thick frost on the ground and you took a full tilt runny only to hit a chuckie (little stone) whereby you were stopped violently in your tracks before slamming your pus off the deck!

Of all the playground Winter Olympic disciplines on offer, throwing snowballs was the Blue Riband event by far. Sconnin someone on the napper and watching it explode was hilarious (and much less destructive than doing it with a stone!). People who wore duffle coats became prime targets due to the fact their jackets were made of wool and, when rattled, the snowball left a mark like a bomb crater. Less funny however was when you got nabbed by a teacher for battering a window or a classmate in the face with a snowball. The outcome was inevitable – a lash on the hand from the teacher's belt. This wasn't a wee thin, soft, fashion belt that kept the teechie's breeks up. Oh no! This was a thick and highly dense piece of leather capable of makkin even the best fighter in the skale greet when administered by certain individuals. The belt was dished out for a wide and varied assortment of offences such as getting nabbed Karate-chopping a ruler in half, farting loudly in class, haein a kerry on or hitting the blackboard with a 'doofer'.

The doofer was a weapon of stealth and was used as a missile to splat off the board, the walls, roof and classmate's heads, all executed of course when the teacher wasn't looking. To make one you simply tore a page from your jotter, or better still, someone else's jotter and rammed the whole lot into your gub then mustered up as much saliva as you could to start chewing. The paper tasted horrendous and was definitely on a par with the taste left in your mouth from licking a window. While on that subject licking batteries was another pastime back then. It was crazy because you knew you were going to get a shock but you still did it. Back to the doofer and for best results, the more you could stomach chewing it, the easier it was to make into a little porridge bomb, very important for sticking purposes. As we got that bit older and moved to secondary school, some of the ultra brave or plain mental pupils would clatter a doofer off the board when the teacher was writing on it. Behaviour like this pushed these nutters right up the rankings and they were usually the kind of people you wanted to stay on the right side of because they obviously couldn't give a monkey's for authority.

Many of these characters were swiftly separated from the flock for being disruptive maniacs and put into what was known then as Remedial Classes. These were set aside to remedy the 'learning difficulties' of these pupils when many were possibly dyslexic and would have benefited far more with channelled techniques for learning in an alternative manner. Add to that possible problems at home and all the ingredients were there for open rebellion.

Sadly, my own father endured the disgraceful attitude taken

by some bullying teachers and went through his whole school life being branded a 'thicko' and told he was useless! My old man can turn his hand to a massive variety of skilled DIY projects, something which the bullies who labelled him could probably never do and yet they called him *thicko*! There are pupils in our schools at present who are hugely talented either musically, artistically and/or physically and are still being let down by an archaic and ignorant system because they can't remember their six times table or spell a word correctly. It is a shocking and disgusting state of affairs in this day and age and the powers that be should hold their empty little heads in shame! (OK, that's the soap box back under meh skale desk – rant over!)

Of course, if you were being an arse in class then you were fair game for a lash or two of the belt.

10

GITTIN THE BELT

The first time I received the belt was in Primary 4 or 5 and I don't remember what the offence was. Our teacher at the time was a male, fairly new to the school and occasionally had the reek of drink on his breath. He also wasn't slow to use his belt. It was utterly humiliating, which in a way was the object I suppose – to be stood out in front of an audience, tried in a kangaroo court then punished. With inch-perfect precision the leather strap met my palm with a crack and sent a pain shooting through me which I'd never experienced before. The worst part of all was the 'walk of shame' back to my seat knowing all eyes in the classroom were fixed on me, waiting for me to crumble.

My hand was stinging like a Box Jellyfish had just sat on it but all I kept saying to myself was 'dinna greet, dinna greet'. Crying in front of everyone would get you labelled a 'right poofter' with a loss of face that would be hard to recover from. Next thing you knew, you'd be shunned from the popular people and end up swapping stamps with the philatelists or mixing with the recorder players (no offence intended to the stamp buffs or wannabe Acker Bilk's out there!). The ironic thing was that if you'd just been thrashed on your writing hand you were expected to pick up your pencil and crack on with the work. This was like asking someone to place their hands in a freezer for an hour then ask them to thread a needle – it was impossible!

There were some laughs though connected with belting. It was always great to see a teacher take a full swing only to miss the pupil's hand and smack the belt off their own leg. It must have been sore as hell but the teacher couldn't show any emotions or the class would have erupted into fits of uproarious laughter. In the circumstances all you could allow yourself was a wee bout of silent mirth and a 'git it up yih!' under your breath. On very rare occasions, one of the really quiet pupils (the ones who never said 'boo' and usually got top marks) was wrongly accused of a crime committed in the class and was given a lash. These poor souls were sometimes crying *before* they even got the belt. Looking back now it was cruel to witness the injustice of that but at the time it was downright hilarious.

By far the best scenario of all was when an individual was brought out to the front for a belting but genuinely believed they had done no wrong and so refused to take the belt. One boy in particular who was a wee waif o a laddie kept holding his hand up when ordered then pulling it away just as the teacher offloaded a full-throttle swing. This was repeated several times and the only thing that had been struck was the teacher's shin and knee – c'mon the peasantry!

I was anything but a rebel at primary and did try my best to stick in and I was only belted a couple of times. However, that all changed at high school! One of the hardest and sorest belts I ever felt was dished out from a female art teacher at Linlathen High School. The class was silent apart from the faint noise of pencils drawing and shading in on pieces of paper. My mate Haze came down from the back of the class for a shot of a rubber and while he was walking back he bawled out 'CAT'S

COBBLERS!' for no apparent reason. Mrs S lifted her head and instantly demanded that the perpetrator make themselves be known. Three of us plus Hazy were holding our sides, crying with laughter as you do at that age. With no-one owning up she decided to keep the four of us behind after the bell for extra questioning in the hope of nailing the upstart. Archie, Haze, Scottie and myself lined up behind her desk as she gave us the third degree and waited for someone to admit responsibility for the outrageous crime. Scottie began rubbing the heels of his Doc Marten shoes together which made a farting noise and that was it – we just burst out laughing in her face!

'Right, you insolent, disgraceful, stupid little boys! If no-one's owning up, you're all getting three of the belt!'

We were still laughing thinking, 'This'll be a breeze,' until she let go on Archie and we saw him wincing. After we all got belted we left her room and instantly put on the 'hard man' act again.

'That wiz a right doddle wiz it?'

'Meh grannie kid belt harder than that!'

'Eh, it wiz like a feather ticklin meh twa palms.'

In truth, we probably all would have liked to be in a dark room alone and scream out, 'OH YA BASTIRD! THAT WIZ SAIR!' But we were *real* men weren't we?

It didn't take you long to suss out the teachers who could deliver maximum pain via the belt and Mrs S could definitely hold her own among the male-dominated top belters. Then there were the others who couldn't belt to save themselves. These were the teachers you knew you could rip the pish out of and any threat of the belt from them was gratefully received. Indeed, it became something of a challenge and whole groups would sometimes set out to deliberately cause mayhem and get a 'tickle on the palm' from these teachers. The peer pressure was overwhelming and anyone not being man enough to get this belt would be slagged off mercilessly. These poor teachers' lives were made hell.

One such teacher hailed from the art department but, thankfully, his belt was a mere brush with a feather compared to Mrs S's 'destroyer'! His class wasn't so much of learning art, it was more like an opportunity to fine tune the skills of mischief and disorder. The same quartet of Scottie, Haze, Archie and me were always up to no good and couldn't really give a shite for shading, landscaping and portrait painting. The four of us ran our operations of chaos and plotted disruption from the back corner.

One day we were working away (quietly for once!) on some pencil drawings when Haze stood up, picked up a rubber from a classmate's desk and launched it at the teacher. Now this rubber was no ordinary rubber. It was called a Big Rub for obvious reasons – it measured about the same size as a breeze block and had enough rubbing power to erase the words from twenty copies of *War and Peace*! This rubber hit the teacher square on the chest like a missile fired from a bazooka and made a painful-sounding dull *'THUMP!'* The most hilarious bit about it was that, without lifting his head and without so much as an 'Ayah!' first, he sternly ordered, 'Archie, get out here now!' whilst reaching into the drawer for his belt. We then erupted into laughter as Archie was off school that day. Poor Mr G just stared despairingly at the three of us as if to say, 'I know one of you bastards did it but I've now made a complete tit of myself!'

He wasn't a bad teacher, in fact, most of us liked him, but he had a hard time controlling us. One day, he went into his cupboard to get something and, before he knew it, the key was turned and he was locked in! Someone eventually decided to open the door and as he came storming out Crookie was standing on a chair waiting for him. He pounced off the chair and right onto Mr G's back where he got him in a stranglehold. The rest of the lads rounded on him and roughed him up a little but it was all taken in good fun if I remember correctly.

At the opposite end of the scale from the 'softie' tutors was a female alpha banshee who flew around Fintry Primary on a broomstick casting evil spells and turning pupils into toads. I'm sure she was originally a sergeant major in the Scots Guards and had an angelic voice that could start an earthquake. Boy could she scream! I thankfully never had the pleasure of her psychotic teaching methods but I recall many a time when some poor bairn was getting it in the ear and her screams raged down the corridor like a verbal pyroclastic blast.

On a more positive note, during those early school days getting a free bottle of milk was something most of us looked forward to. The teacher would designate a couple of bodies to put the straws in the bottles then dish them out to the class. This was a great little perk because there were usually a couple of spare bottles left over in the crate and the helpers would get these extras. Margaret Thatcher was the Secretary of State for Education and Science under Ted Heath's Conservative government during the early 1970s and she and her cronies infamously abolished free milk in primary schools. I'm not sure how this affected us because I still remember getting milk around 1978. Some of the poorer pupils also received free meals which was a little embarrassing for them because classmates instantly knew their parents didn't have the money and they were labelled 'minks' or 'tinkies' unless of course they were hard as nails and you'd get your pus rapped for such an assassination of character!

GITTIN THE BELT

Back then, the majority of pupils went to school dinners and the rest went home. I did both and I must confess, for the most part, I actually enjoyed school dinners, especially the thick, lumpy custard and the square of cake which was usually mashed into a sweet pulp. There was no messing about; the grub was scoffed up rapidly so you could get back out to play. The whole culture of kids going to shops outside of school and buying a pile of saturated fat-laden crap was still years away. There was hardly anybody you could have classed as fat and the odd one or two who were slightly plump were labelled with the undesirable handle of 'Fatty'. In today's obese climate they would have been considered 'highly toned athletes' and if things keep going the way they're going, skinny pupils will be in the minority and the ones taking a slagging.

Sports Day for many of us was the highlight of the primary school calendar and was held near the end of term. These were the days when it was it was acceptable, indeed *encouraged* to be competitive among your fellow pupils. It was of course an opportunity to see where you were in the class and school pecking order and also where exactly you figured in the 'cool' stakes. This last point was very important when trying to impress a girl you fancied and wanted to 'go with'. If you could compliment that with getting into the school football team, being able to make girls laugh and be a good scrapper, you were head and shoulders above the rest and well on your way. I was fairly good at the sports and the football but talking to girls scared the living daylights out of me and I couldn't fight my way out of a wet paper bag, although I made out to my mates I could.

As for the Sports Day itself, there was no mercy or quarter given for the plump, the backward or the disabled. When that whistle blew to start the race, whether it was the sprint, the

91

rope hurdles or the egg and spoon race it was a case of 'up you lot – ehm gonna win this an eh couldna gie a monkey's if Fatty's waddlin in last!'

Of course that evolutionary, genetic and instinctive form of human thinking is slowly being crushed by the small band of politically correct fuds who nowadays want to make everyone taking part a 'winner'. What a load of shite!

Something which didn't lose its true competitive edge in the playground was scrapping. Fights between pupils could explode instantaneously over the least little thing or could be a pre-planned square-go between two combatants who'd had a slight disagreement and had decided to sort the matter out in a gentlemanly fashion. Personally, I don't remember many boxing matches at primary school. A lot of the fights would begin with two bodies squaring up to each other, then a load of verbals with challenges like, 'Mon then!', 'Hink yir hard?', 'Ir you startin?' This was backed up with physical gestures such as arms being splayed apart in challenge, sticking out the chest and pulling the shoulders back or forcing the head forward from the neck. A tit-for-tat shoving match would start where the shoves would gradually build up in force until someone got fed up and either backed down or grabbed their opponent's hair and attempted to pull them down to get a few kicks into their head. I never fully understood the philosophy behind that last move as it was nigh on impossible to kick someone's head from that position and range. Sometimes both pupils would grab the hair at the same time and would be locked in this clinch for ages before mutually calling it quits and brushing all the clumps of hair from their hands.

The best fights were when one of the recognised 'good' scrappers claimed another of the good scrappers to sort out a wee power struggle. As soon as someone uttered the magic words 'You're claimed!' the adrenaline was on. Supporters would take sides and the scrap was usually scheduled for 'hame time'. The strange thing was, the location of the square-go was commonly pre-determined and agreed by both fighters, i.e. on the grass or on the concrete. Word went around the school like wild fire and often huge numbers of pupils would gather to watch the bout.

Something which I didn't understand at the time and still don't understand now was when the crowd started spitting on the people scrapping. This could be on the person getting beaten or occasionally on both. It was disgusting to see fellow pupils covered from head to toe in gochuls (saliva). It was very noticeable however, that this kind of nonsense never happened when the top boys went into action. I recall a fight between two of the older pupils – a P6 and a P7 when it was alleged they were both 'tooled up'. Being younger, there was no way you were getting a front seat for the bout but I still remember the Deputy Head, Miss D, coming to split the scrap up and she ended up allegedly looking for a knife which had been chucked under the Mobile Hut. The other lad had been using a belt and buckle. This all came as a bit of a shock, the thought of someone actually carrying a blade in school! The ironic thing was that the shops sold these little penknives to kids with various lengths of blade and a tartan handle. With knife crime in some areas currently reaching dangerously high levels it seems absolutely preposterous to think that weapons would be available for children to buy without so much as an eyebrow being raised. For the record, I only ever had a couple of minor skirmishes at primary school and much preferred to have a laugh. I knew roughly where I was in the pack and it suited me just fine.

One of the most discomforting memories from the school

days had to be the painful task of going for a dump. The fact you had to go into a cubicle in the first place was pretty horrible as your mates would wait till the moment when your breeks were at your ankles and you were at your most vulnerable then lob handfuls of water and wet paper towels over the walls and soak you. If that wasn't bad enough, once you'd had your dump, you were expected to wipe with Izal toilet paper and not cry. Whoever invented this stuff must have been a right sadistic bastard. It was like wiping your arse with broken glass. In fact, wiping was the wrong term, it was more like smearing. It resembled tracing paper and had no absorbing qualities whatsoever. Worse still, my gran worked there as a cleaner and used to nick this stuff which meant I was treated to a double helping of arse lacerations. She also used to nick huge blocks of carbolic soap – using it was like washing yourself with a breeze block. Oh, they were tough times!

Another equally (albeit differently administered!) painful experience was getting a 'wedgie'. I didn't know what the hell it was until a few days into Secondary School when I saw a poor little fellow First Year suffer one from some older pupils. He was sobbing uncontrollably and no bloody wonder! The arse of his Y-Fronts was just about touching his neck which meant he probably had a split scrotum and an inflated bollock on each hip! Sooner or later you'd get one but thankfully, mine wasn't severe. The worst one of all was a 'double wedgie' when a mob of bullying gangsters would grab the front and rear ends of the undies and lift the victim into the air. These 'doublers' could turn boys into instant eunuchs!

It was imperative that you went into school each morning and remained totally switched on for the course of the day as people were constantly trying to maim you for a laugh. This worked both ways but you never dared try it on a hard man. A common ploy was to ask someone to smell the palm of their hand and as they did so, you'd slam your hand onto theirs and nearly annihilate their nose. Also, it paid to be wary when talking to someone and they began smirking for no apparent reason. If you weren't alert, a boy would kneel down on all fours behind you and the decoy would then shove you and cause you to fall violently over them. Worst case scenario was having your hands in your pockets and being pushed over on concrete. There was a very real danger of smashing your skull but it was funny when it was someone else getting shoved.

Being punctual and getting to school on time was very important back then and any slip up would possibly result in a lash from the belt. Apart from the few screwballs and the odd lunatic, most of us showed a healthy respect to our teachers, certainly at primary anyway. When they blasted their whistle or raised their voices you took notice. In saying that, there was still room for episodes of nonsense and shenanigans. One of the all-time classics was to put a drawing pin on a classmate's seat and wait for them to sit on it. This was hilarious to witness as the victim would always first let out a scream then shift their arse upwards at lightning speed. It was only a matter of time though before your own arse was punctured and the laughter was reversed. The important lesson here was not to grass or clipe on anyone. It was one of the fundamental laws of the street which you learned early doors. There were a few wolves however, who would hide amongst the flock and couldn't wait to drop you in the shite at the first opportunity.

'Miss, Miss, Jimmy's copying meh answers an ee says if eh grass then ehm 'gittin it' at hame time Miss!'

'Well then Jimmy had better get out here to the floor and we'll see if the strap changes his attitude a little.'

'Yih wee turd yih!'

The teacher used to have a big bulky pencil sharpener clamped to their desk and this lent itself to having a wee kerry on when they weren't looking and you could make daft faces at your mates. A six inch pencil would slowly be ground down to two inches but with a point the size of a knitting needle! Getting nabbed capering like this would probably warrant the reduced sentence of having to stand in the back corner of the class and 'face the wall'. If the offence was committed early on you were in for a hellishly long shift! I remember an incident at Greenfield Primary when I'd just sharpened a pencil to the same sharpness as a needle and thought it would be cool to hold the pointed end with my bottom lip and 'bounce' it across the desk. My fellow pupils looked rather impressed until the fourth attempt when there was no bounce. It had been replaced with a loud scream as the pencil went right through my bottom lip and stuck. After a wee stint of crying like a fairy the teacher pulled it out and it was back on with the work – no risk assessment forms to fill out, no ambulance to the DRI, no phoning of the parents while they're at work to come and collect their 'injured little angel', no suing of the teacher, the makers of the pencil or the offending sharpener. No, it was the good old British 'stiff upper lip again' (or lower lip in my case) and 'crack on old chap' – the way it should be!

Farting in class was a risky affair as the teacher didn't find that sort of behaviour funny in the slightest. It took a lot of bottle to let one go but the results were phenomenal. The hard surface of the plastic or wooden seats meant you got a real ripper which went down great with rest of the class. You only hoped the teacher didn't nab you or you were in for it. Later, at high school, this was taken a whole step further during exams when there were around two hundred pupils sitting in the gym hall. Once the first bomb reverberated around the place the flatulent concerto began and the great thing was there was no way of getting caught. I must stress however that this was purely a lad's thing and don't want to tar the girls with the same brush. In all my years at school I don't ever recall a girl dropping one.

No doubt everyone will remember the occasions when some unfortunate classmate was sick and hoyed up in the class. You could just about taste the stench, it was absolutely mingin. It was quite an event and broke up the day as we waited on the jannie appearing with the infamous bucket of sawdust to spread over the pizza of human bile. What the hell was that all about? Surely, the more sensible course of action would have been to remove the diced-carrot blancmange and gie the flair a good scrub wi' disinfectant!

Even worse though was when some poor sod pished their breeks in the class. The slagging they took wasn't anywhere near as humiliating as when they had to visit the Auxiliary Nurse and were handed a pair of trousers or a pinafore from the 1940s to wear for the rest of the day.

I don't ever remember our jannie having a real name. To us he was affectionately known as 'Kipper-hade' but Christ knows what that was all about. His head looked nothing like a fish! He also got 'Egg-hade' or 'Eggo' due to his lack of hair. He was a thin wee baldy man with a pair of bandy legs and was about ninety-six years old (or so he seemed to us!). We saw him as just another 'grumpy aald codger' who spoiled our fun of playing on the school roof at night or crashing a ball off the school windows. Along with a whole multitude of others in the scheme we conspired to making this poor man's life complete hell with relentless taunts of 'Awa yih baldy aald bastird!' and 'Eggo, yir a slap-hade!' He'd probably survived two World Wars, the Boer War and the Crimea and been decorated with enough medals to fill a whole tunic and there we were, a bunch of cheeky little upstarts ripping the pish out of him. Mr Jannie . . . if you're *up there* and can hear me, I apologise from the bottom of my heart and will get you a pint when I get *up there* with you.

The happiest memory of all my primary school days was being picked to play for the school football team. For me, that would always top getting straight A passes in exams or being the 'head boy', not that I was *EVER* going to be in the running for that accolade. In our circles it wasn't cool to be a swot or play the tuba or the clarinet. For the majority of us scheme boys, football was the be all and end all and nothing else mattered in life. From just about the moment I could stand, my old man had me kicking a ball and pretty soon after that all I wanted to be was a footballer.

I was very lucky in the fact that I usually had a ball and practiced my skills constantly, even learning to play with my 'bad' left foot. It's funny to think back that only one or two of us in the squad had a ball and sometimes they were the cheap, blow away type but it didn't really matter as long as you could get a game of football. These days, you'll often pass a garden with maybe two or three fancy leather Adidas or Nike balls lying around. Years ago they would have been knocked fae the gairden as soon as they were left unattended, such was the scarcity of owning a good ball. I remember my dad had a Pools coupon win which amounted to a massive, life-changing £3.84 win, or it was to me because he bought me my first ever brand new tub (leather ball). I couldn't stop staring at it and smelling it on the bus journey home. The white hexagonal panels mesmerised me and I fell into a trance of total worship. If I could have framed it, I would have and hung it on my bedroom wall. When I did finally let it out to be used as a football, it was only allowed onto the softest and most luscious green grass and I even felt guilty having to kick it. The ball was carried everywhere and I was very reluctant to let it out of my grasp when someone shouted, 'Hey Roabee, geeza touch o yir ba?'

'Eh, well ok, but mind – nae kickin it on the concrete, yull scratch it!' Predictably, it would eventually stray out of the player's control and onto the stone. 'Aw fir fuck's sake, eh telt yih tih keep it aff the pavey yih prick!' This mollycoddling behaviour lasted about a week before it was getting toed off the shop shutters and booted off harling walls and ended up skinless.

One of the great memories for me was doing a running commentary as if you were David Coleman commentating on a big match on TV. You'd put on a 'commentator's voice' and talk yourself and your mates through the moves, gradually building into a frenzied finish (if you scored that is!).

'Yes, here he is, it's Souness on the ball, gliding gracefully through the midfield, carefully avoiding the lump of dog shite on the park. He looks up, passes out wide to John Robertson. Robertson shimmies, leaps over a sliding tackle and finds Dalglish unmarked in the box. Dalglish controls beautifully, picks his spot and lashes an unstoppable pile-driver into the roof of the net. It's 4-nil and Scotland are annihilating the English. The World Cup is coming home to Scottish soil and the English kin git it right up thum!'

In school, we played both playtimes and a big match at dinner time. The games were mostly class versus class and were very hotly contested. No-one wanted to play in goal so the crapiest player would be shoved in and expected to keep a clean sheet. Everyone wanted to score which resulted in a huge mob from both sides chasing the ball. The posts were marked with a jumper or a jacket but due to the number of players lobbing their garments down, each post sometimes measured three feet across. Arguments would erupt before the game had even kicked off if one team suspected the others' posts weren't the same distance apart, thus giving them an advantage. The height of the 'invisible' bar was a complete lottery.

'Oh yih dancer, wut a GOAL!'

'Awa an shite, that wiz ower!'

'Nae danger, the keeper coulda touched that, it wiz fuckin IN!' And so the dispute raged until both sides reluctantly agreed one way or the other or a compromise was reached and a penalty was awarded as an alternative. As the game was refereed without a ref, anything and everything was claimed for. Hacking and kicking the hell out of someone's shins rarely resulted in a foul with aggressive retaliation the only means of compensation. Occasionally, a three-rounder would explode and fists and boots would start flying for one wayward tackle too many.

Trials were held for the school football team for Primary 6s and 7s but on rare occasions a laddie from Primary 5 would make the team because of his exceptional skills. One of the happiest days of my whole schooling career was seeing my name on the 'selected' list for the team when I was still in Primary 6. Mr L (who was a Scottish volleyball internationalist) ran the team and was one of those teachers who were firm but also fair. He was a good man and encouraged us all wholeheartedly while sharing a good bit of banter and a laugh. Although we had a load of good players in the team such as Darren B, Davie B and Scott B, we were often gubbed and bucked a trend from previous years when the school had been spoilt for choice with an abundance of exceptionally talented players. Guys like future Rangers and Scotland star Derek Johnstone, Dundee United's John Reilly and Charlie Adam senior, who was to star for a host of Scottish clubs, all graced the ranks of Fintry Primary's school team. And there were many, many others with tremendous skill who were part of the team's success. We brought a crashing halt to all that and won bugger all.

The winter months were a nightmare as you had to change at the side of the park with no protection from the elements. Sometimes your fingers would get so cold you couldn't get your shirt buttons done up or the zip o yir breeks pulled up. Playing for the team did of course have one great perk – on the day of the match you got away from lessons in the afternoon. Occasionally, Haze would get himself into bother in the class and our teacher wouldn't let him away for the game which was a bummer because we needed him. We never won any silverware or gained any medals but we did have a great time trying.

11

THE FAIRER SEX

As a young lad I never paid too much attention to girls. They merely got in the way of doing 'boy's things' and having a carry on, plus they couldn't play football so that was that. Having a younger sister was more than enough contact with the female species for me. To put it bluntly, she got right on my tits and more often than not, we ended up fighting like hell. Most of the scraps erupted after school when we were in the house alone until our parents finished work. She'd be watching one channel on TV and I'd want to watch another. Before long we were bawling and shouting and tearing lumps from each other. The end result was always the same, she'd be locked in the bathroom until the old lady or old man came home and then I'd get scattered or if I was lucky, we'd both get scattered.

The one thing my old man looked forward to when he got home from work (when he went to it that is!) was a wee bit of peace and quiet while he scoffed his tea. There was no danger of that though when me and Steff got started. We'd be fighting over nothing and the noise would get louder and louder. The old man was pretty fair and would bark a few warnings before the cutlery got slammed on the table and you knew you were in for a leathering.

I blame my sister (obviously, because I'm writing this!). Her moaning voice always attracted the old man's attention and we were done for. If she had learned to scrap quietly we wouldn't have received half of the tankings we got. We had a few cracking bouts and as I was the oldest she evened things up by using weapons. One time we were arguing at the dinner table and she stuck a fork in my nut. I went to skelp her back and knocked a full plate of tomato soup right up the wall. That went down great with the old man! During another set-to she stuck a sewing pin deep into my forearm. And then there were the ornamental breakages and damage to furniture which we'd blame each other for. Ultimately, the both of us got skelped.

I remember stealing some magnesium ribbon from chemistry class so I could conduct some experiments of my own. This stuff was highly flammable and dangerous, which is why I knocked it. Unknown to me, Steff found it in my room and decided to light it – in the house! She panicked when it burst into life and threw it onto the recently purchased new carpet, burning a few dirty great holes in it. She got scattered for the burning and I got scattered for bringing the bloody stuff home!

We often laugh with our parents now when we think back how wild some of the fights were. Like I say, when you heard the old man's cutlery crashing it was time to take off, not that you were going to get very far. You'd take off upstairs but the old man would easily make the ground up taking four stairs at a time. After a good skelp he'd head back down stairs and out of earshot, or so you thought.

'Eh, yih big poof!'

'*WUT DID YOU SAY?*' Three bounds and he was right back up.

'Naw, naw, eh sade mih ba's on the *roof!*' WAHLUP!

Steff got the tanking of a lifetime from my mum once when

she mistakenly did a few minor adjustments to a pair of my trousers. I had an old pair of black jeans which were too small for me so I told Steff she could have them and just to take them from my cupboard as I had got new ones. She gladly accepted this rare gift of brotherly love and set about cutting six inches off the legs and sewing a neat little hem on them. A few days later I went searching for the new black jeans which my old lady had just paid a whopping fourteen quid for. They weren't hanging where they should have been but what *was* still hanging there was the old pair. Then the penny dropped and I realised my sister had made a monumental blunder and cut the brand new jeans.

'Mither! Yull no believe it! She's went an cut mih new jeans up!' She went completely off her rocker and began screaming and cursing at my sister then set about her like a woman possessed. Eventually, I had to haul my old lady off and calm her down. Fourteen quid was a lot of money out of the family budget. Steff did well out of it, after the initial doing anyway, and got herself a brand new pair o troosers!

As for taking an interest in girls, I was a very slow starter and was too busy wandering around in my own wee world. I was also very shy when it came to speaking to members of the fairer sex. That's not to say I didn't take any notice of girls. When we were at Fintry Primary School and had a gym class sometimes we'd get to use the communal showers. They were slap bang in the middle of the boys' and girls' changing rooms and boys being boys, there would be a bit of a wrestling match to get a look through the keyhole and watch the girls.

'Oh yih fucker, eh jist seen so-and-so's pud!'

'Wut wiz it like? Is it a big hairy ane?'

'Oh, an there's sumdeez erse!'

'C'mon, you've been there fir ages, geeza look yih prick!'

The term used for this kind of behaviour was 'gittin yir chaipirz' which basically translates to 'getting cheap thrills'. This was all fine and well and caused much giggling among us until a suspicious teacher burst into the room and usually caught someone with their eyeball glued to the keyhole, then there was hell to pay. Showering with the lads had absolutely nothing in comparison to watching the girls shower and there was always one numpty who thought it was highly amusing to pish all over your legs.

There was, however, a much easier way of getting chaipirz and that was to ask to stay up late on a Friday night and watch the late horror film with the old man. He was probably staying up for the same reason I was, although he wouldn't admit it. The Hammer horror films nearly always had a glimpse of some female bits at some point. What this had to do with the story God only knows but it probably threw the viewing figures up tenfold. I'd be lying on the couch following the story intently, scared to go upstairs on my own when the mood would change unexpectedly, but pleasantly. Off would drop a female vampire's negligee to reveal a large pair of heaving breasts. Quality family entertainment!

Sunday nights were eagerly anticipated too and you'd time getting out of your once-weekly bath to coincide with the *Tales of the Unexpected* series coming on telly. The opening credits were graced with the brief silhouette of a voluptuous female dancing around erotically. The programme was a huge hit in the late '70s but I don't think this was down to the great storylines. The *real* reason I suspect was everyone was waiting for the dancing dame to come on again at the end credits.

The first girl I ever took a fancy to was Diana Smith, who was in my class at Fintry, but I don't think she was ever aware of my interest as I never had the bottle to tell her. I used to get a

105

little flutter of butterflies in my stomach when I saw her coming down the road to school, walking with her pal Helena. This would have been around the time I was in Primary 4 or 5. Instead of plucking up the courage to speak to her I'd try and impress her by running past her at high speed or if we weren't playing football and actually playing with the girls, I'd always 'tig' her or catch her at chase-ays. This did nothing to impress her and probably planted the view in her head that I was some kind of stalker.

Running through girls' strings of elastics and snapping them or jumping into their skipping rope games was also used as a form of flirting but had the opposite effect of enamouring you with the girls and only succeeded in them branding you an 'arsehole'. It was all very innocent and part of the early learning curve of striking up a friendly relationship with a member of the opposite sex. Even if a girl had said, 'Yes, I like you and I'd like to be your girlfriend,' it would have been pretty much in verbal terms only.

Holding a girl's hand (even one you really liked!) in front of anyone and especially your mates, would have earned you a 'big poofy sissy' handle which would have stuck for the rest of your school days. A kiss? That would have been out of the question! One peck on the cheek and she may have ended up pregnant! I think it's fair to say that we were all still of an age where naivety and innocence ruled and although we maybe liked to make out we knew what 'dirty words' meant, in all honesty we didn't have a clue.

As you got that wee bit older and took a fraction more of an interest in the opposite sex, the whole business of pairing up became distinctly complicated. Speaking directly to the one you 'fancied' was still a long way off so the connection was made via one of your mates or a friend of the 'fancied one'.

THE FAIRER SEX

This was done mostly at school in the playground. After much deliberating and plucking up courage you'd let the cat out of the bag and ask this mate to go and, 'Ask if shull go wi' is?' To 'go where?' I never quite got to the bottom of but it was the standard question everyone asked. This was a very dodgy and tricky operation and your heart would pump like crazy as you watched your mate stroll over to the group where the apple of your eye stood. Sometimes the excited anticipation would turn to horror as he approached the wrong girl. Helplessly, you'd watch as he struck up a dialogue then start pointing over to where you were. Even from afar, you could read the lips.

'Eh, mih mate ower there's askin if yull go wi' uhm?'

'Wah *HIM?* Nah, eh dinna hink so. No in a mullion years!'

He'd be looking over, shaking his head and it was pretty obvious his lips were saying, 'Shih says nut!' This was all bad enough but if she was one of the not-so-bonnie girls then you'd have to leave the country immediately because in less than ten seconds the whole school would know you'd had a 'knock back' from her! Equally crushing was getting a knock back from the proper girl as you then knew she wasn't interested in the slightest in you.

I think the first time I got a proper kiss on the lips was at my tenth birthday party. Mind you, it *was* during a game of Postman's Knock but it was a start. I'm sure the next one for me was on my eighteenth! You'd hear of guys who'd advanced to the dizzy heights of 'necking' and maybe even a 'feelee', or at least that's what they said they'd done! I used to wonder what it would be like to neck a girl and would try to simulate the action with myself in the bathroom mirror.

The whole lead up to puberty was a complete nightmare as there was no guidebook or instructor showing you just what was expected. The first neckie for most young folk is just a slavering shambles made worse by the dilemma of 'do you go for it and stick your tongue into her gub and risk a slap in the pus and getting packed up?'

Opportunities of a different kind presented themselves at the local community-centre discos. Free from the school environment, attitudes were slightly more relaxed and open and boys and girls would gather in their own little groups with some showing an interest in certain individuals. If you were feeling really brave you'd relay via messenger again that you'd like to do a 'moonie' with a girl you fancied. Younger readers might think this involved the both of you dropping your drawers and baring your arses at everyone but it was nothing of the sort. It was a dance and a slow one at that where you both experienced possibly the first ever physical contact with a boy or a girl. Sometimes you both stood awkwardly at arm's length with hands on each other's shoulders and just swayed monotonously sidewards in the same spot for the duration of a record whilst staring shyly into space. Other times it was magical. The two of you approach each other, faces momentarily lit up by the coloured lights from the rotating disco ball. The mood is perfect as the DJ plays David Soul's 'Don't Give Up On Us Baby'. Eyes meet and smiles are exchanged and hands softly rest on each other's waist. The rest of the world doesn't exist.

'Fuck me, eh am in love! This is it, ehm gonna merry this lassie as soon as wir baith sixteen.'

'Snap oot o it yih eedeeit! Wir goin awa backie hoppin efter here.'

'Oh eh, eh firgot. Right, that's the weddin aff then!'

Strangely, this sort of slow dancing with girls and showing some natural emotion was acceptable among the lads but what was totally *unacceptable* was having a casual dance with a girl to a song such as 'Angelo' by Brotherhood Of Man. You would have had the pish ripped out of you and called a gaybob. Casual dancing with the fairer sex was regarded as grossly improper and poofy. Ironically, what *was* tolerable was dancing with rest of the boys to Northern Soul or pogoing about to punk music. But that was different – that was manly bonding with fellow scheme warriors.

It was a similar situation to when boys began getting their ears pierced. The unwritten rule was one earring only and I'm sure it had to be worn in the left ear. Anyone caught wearing it in the wrong ear or worse still, one in each ear, would have been as well changing their name to Danny La Rue and wearing a pink frock!

Sadly, one of the best forms of housing scheme sex education has all but disappeared from our streets and parks. There's either a severe lack of dirty old men going about these days or trends have changed. Finding a discarded scud book (or books) was the nearest thing a young boy was going to get to sex education. Editions such as *Fiesta* and *Mayfair* showed the female anatomy in all its naked and semi-naked glory. All the main bits were clearly shown. The more explicit magazines showed how it was done and what positions could be achieved with a little creativity.

I remember a mate and I found one of these explicit jobs not far from his house but instead of taking it away to a 'safe area' for inspection, excitement got the better of us and we delved right in about it where we found it and began turning the pages excitedly. Unfortunately, we were unaware that his dad had nipped out to the shops. On his return he literally stumbled across us giggling nervous laughs and pointing to areas of interest. Our sex education class ended abruptly as the mag was grabbed and my mate was frogmarched over to his house for a roond o the guns and a few Wahlups!

Probably the most monumentally embarrassing moment from my early attempts at chivalry and actually talking to a female I fancied came when I approached this girl one night after the carnival at Caird Park. Another of the phrases in circulation at the time was 'gittin awa wi' sumdee' or translated: getting away with a person romantically. I didn't have a clue what this really meant or what it entailed. Much later I found out that it ranged from kissing to necking, feeleez to heavy petting and in very, very rare cases – more! In my naive and innocent mind, for all I knew 'gittin awa wi' a lassie' could easily have been 'escapin fae the Fuzz wi' a female accomplice efter pannin a windee in'. To put things into perspective, I was still playing Subbuteo at fifteen when many lads the same age were getting pished on Merrydown cider, sniffing glue and thinking of ways to get their leg over with someone. The simple solution to this lack of knowledge would have been to ask someone but that would have told everyone else that you didn't have a clue about things of a sexual nature and thrown you right into the chess and clarinet players category again.

Anyway, back to 'carnival girl' and the red face I was about to wear. I'd made the decision beforehand that if I saw her, there would be no holding back – 'Eh wiz gonna git awa wi' ir!' What I never realised was that to reach that advanced stage, a relationship was usually constructed over a period of time with meaningful dialogue and getting to know the person. I skipped all that nonsense and therefore didn't pass GO and didn't collect £200 a-la-Monopoly! The adrenaline raced through my body in an explosive torrent as I approached, loaded the verbal bullets, then pulled the trigger.

'Wahr ih wih goin?'

'Wut?' was her reply. She had a strange and very confused look on her face. On seeing this, the alarm bells started ringing and I began to crumble from the inside out. My conversation opener had obviously puzzled her. As we knew each other fairly well she probably expected a greeting along the lines of, 'Hey, how's it going? Did you have a good night at the carnival? Would you mind if I walked you home and we can chat along the way? Your hair looks different tonight, I really like it . . .'

My expectations following my opener were somewhat different to those. I visualised her putting her arm around me, cuddling in tightly, kissing me passionately then softly saying in my ear, 'Where would *you* like to go?' In reality, there followed what seemed like a two-hour awkward silence before I half smiled, let out a pathetically nervous whimper then turned and walked away, my confidence utterly destroyed. Any further attempts at the dating game were duly abandoned. I did however find solace in my index finger during the hard months and years which followed and became shit-hot at Subbuteo!

12

WUTZ THE GEMME?

I was lucky enough to grow up in the generation where making your own fun and playing games was expected of you while the adults got on with the adult things. You were encouraged to use your imagination, be creative and play both on your own and as part of a group. If you'd dared mutter the words, 'Ehm bored!' or, 'Thirz nuhin tih dae!' you would have earned yourself a thick ear and that was just for starters. The other reason you made your own fun was money, or rather the lack of it. The only occasions when you received gifts was for birthdays and Christmas's and whether they were big or small, you certainly learned to appreciate what you were given.

The games we played in the schemes were a mixture of ones passed down through the years and newer ones which some forward-thinking young pioneers had invented. The first and obvious one for most boys was football and all the nonsense described earlier with jackets for posts, the height of the bar, etc. As well as the football, a whole load of other games were played, many of these at school while some also transported to the streets out of school hours.

One of the first games I remember playing when I moved to Fintry Primary school was called *Hoppy Christie*. This was played out in the shelter or the 'Sheddie' as it was commonly known and involved a single person on each side of the building hopping over to one another with folded arms and barging together aggressively in an attempt to make the opponent drop a leg and win. It sometimes got out of hand when you caught a fly elbow in the face, where you'd retaliate back in kind.

Toy Fighting was another early learner and was self explanatory – get your mate down and beat the hell out of him (in a friendly manner of course!). The other kind of 'fighting' was re-enacting battles between either Cowboys and Indians or Japs and Jerries. The latter one I never fully understood as to the best of my knowledge, the Japanese and the Germans never ever had a scrap with each other. A few of us would link arms in the playground then go around kicking our legs out like a chorus line from a Broadway classic and sing, 'Wahz waant a gemme at Japs an Jerries?' More and more boys would join until you had a couple of armies ready to wage war. This was great fun with anything up to twenty wee laddies running about with imaginary guns, making firing noises and slaughtering the enemy. Arguments would often flare up when somebody wouldn't 'play dead' after being obviously mown down in a hail of 'invisible rounds' from a Sten gun.

'Eh shot you yih prick!'

'Nah yih didna, yih missed coz eh got cover behind that bushy. An anyweh, eh wid've felt it yih balloon!'

'Ach, yoor a chaitin bastird! Eh killed yih an yir *stull* waanderin aboot? Yih widna be daein that in a *right* battle!'

'Ach, wull yih git aff yir hegh horse you? Yir only a corporal an yir goin aboot there like a general!'

The best place to play these battles was in a location where there were plenty of hidey-holes and natural barricades. It wasn't long before you perfected the skills of weapons handling and became adept in the arts of ambush, urban and jungle warfare. Sticks were transformed into sniper rifles, machine guns, bazookas and samurai swords. One of the most sought after and prized of weapons was only available in certain areas at certain times. The 'sand-bomb' could only be obtained from a garden where the earth had been dug up or hoed and then dried in the sun. These 'grenades' would explode on impact, giving off a puff of smoke and were capable of killing at least six enemy soldiers.

Continuing on the war theme, we used to play a game called *Dade Man's Fa* or 'Dead Man's Fall'. A group of you would line up in front of one person who stood a short distance away and who would then ask each of you in turn what kind of weapon you'd like to be killed with. Every man would try to outdo the previous with an over-the-top theatrical dying act. The choice of weapons would begin in standard fashion before quickly progressing to the realms of ridiculous.

'Right Tam, wut dih yih waant?'

'Ehl hae a rifle.' The shot was fired and down you'd go, just like you'd seen in the *Guns of Navarone*.

'Right, nixt?'

'Gie me a poisoned dart fae a blowpipe.' A horrible and painfully slow death would follow until it started to get out of hand.

'Geeza flamethrower follyed beh standin on a tank mine.'

'Ehl hae an atom bomb.' The acting was very creative and played to a tremendously high standard.

Choosing teams or individual people to be a chaser or such was usually settled by a unique little method which was fair and saved arguments as to who teamed up with who, etc. Everyone involved would gather together and place a foot into a circle then someone would say a little ditty. Each foot would be tapped during the saying or spelling of words in the ditty, for example: 'Dic-dic-tation-cor-por-a-tion, how-many-buses-are-in-the-sta-tion?' The finger would come to rest on a foot and that person would say a number which in turn was spelt out. Whoever's foot the finger finally landed on was either chosen to be on a team or unfortunately, they were the person chosen to be 'oot' and had to catch everyone. It was never fun being oot! Another of these dittys went, 'My-mother-punched-your-mother-right-in-the-pus-and-guess-what-colour-the-blood-was? The colour could be anything from yellow to magenta to tartan and again this was spelt out as above. Yet another one had all the participants gathered in a circle and holding out both fists. Someone was designated counter and bumped their own fists onto everyone else's while saying 'One-potato-two-potato-three-potato-four-five-six-seven-more.' Whoever the rhyme ended on put a fist away and so it continued until both were gone. Probably, one of the most common and widely used actions for deciding who was out etc was the old 'Stane, Paper and Scissors' routine with the hands.

Games like *Tig, High Tig, Underarm Tig, Hide and Seek* and *Roondirz* (Rounders) were old classics and run-of-the-mill as were *British Bulldogs* and *Reelee-fo*. The rules of the latter two are sketchy now but if memory serves me correctly the game would begin with one person trying to catch another as a whole group ran from one point across to another. This would continue until the last person (who was nearly always the fastest runner) was caught.

Two Man Hunt as the name suggests, consisted of two people hunting others down one-by-one until everyone was caught, which meant being physically grabbed and not just spotted. This particular game could often last for hours when played at night, for the two men hunting anyway. Even though boundaries had been agreed beforehand, people sometimes buggered off home without telling the poor hunters, who were left trawling the scheme for ages before eventually realising they'd had the mickey taken out of them.

Wak The Plank or Jine The Crew? was without doubt the roughest of all the games we played. One or two boys were crew members to start off and it was their job to round up mutineers and pressgang them into joining the crew. If these lads were fairly soft, the chances of joining the crew were very remote but if one of the better fighters in your year offered his services then the severity of walking the plank became serious. On your capture, the crew would shout the words: 'Wak the plank or jine the crew?'

'Ach git it up yiz, ehl wak the plank!' As soon as you'd said that – BANG! You were clobbered then wrestled to the ground and given a few digs to make you capitulate. The question was asked again to see if your resolve had weakened any.

'Nah, uhm no giein in.'

'Right gie uhm a Chinese burn!'

For anyone who never experienced one of these, your wrist was grabbed and two hands turned either way to twist your skin causing a serious friction burn.

'Arite, uhl jine, uhl jine yih bastirdz!'

The Chinese burn was a finisher as was the 'piley on'. The latter could be anything up to seven or eight bodies piling on top of you. With that kind of weight, it's fair to say you thought you were going to die! Sometimes you had to use a little tact and 'jine the crew' straight away following capture as there were a few maniacs waiting to administer some *real* pain!

Playing *Chickenelly* was great fun but also had an element of danger with it. Funny how your young mind worked and you found it hilarious to know that a knock at the door had forced the householder out of their comfy chair to answer, only to find there was nobody there – brilliant! Not so brilliant though were the times when a man came flying out and gave chase shouting threats of, 'Ehl brack yir fuckin legs yih wee bastirdz!' As soon as someone like this took the bait you'd end up going back night after night and pestering the hell out of them. When there was a group of you doing the chappin, once the door was rattled, you'd all take off in riotous order. No-one wanted to be left at the back, especially when some psychopath was on your heels and occasionally, dirty tricks would come into play where the gate would be closed on the last man. If the householder nabbed them they were in for a hefty boot in the arse.

On the subject of getting chased, our small band of rebel rousers had two episodes in particular where getting caught for our actions simply wasn't an option. The first one occurred on a beautifully sunny and slightly snowy winter's day when we were off school for the Christmas holidays and at a loose end. Mac, Haze, Sean and me were wandering about wondering what we could do to entertain ourselves when someone had a brainwave – a moment of inspired genius.

'Litz see iff wih kin git some sna ba's right in Fawlty's doorway.'

This was in Findhorn Street and not far from Haze's house. Nowadays, these houses look like solid, stone-built dwellings but underneath the harling coat lies the old metal structures. They really were strange houses which looked like they'd been built using Meccano sets. They were on two levels with one family occupying the ground floor and the other living upstairs. 'Fawlty' as you may have gathered, was a ringer for the character from Fawlty Towers. The upstairs dwellers' door sat

117

at the top of a flight of stairs on the gable end and Fawlty had stupidly left his open. In our eyes this was a natural target practice opportunity not to be missed. The four of us stood lobbing these snowballs into his loabee (hallway) for ages. The bottom landing must have been overflowing with snow but still we kept raining down our frozen missiles. Quite a few went wide of the mark and clattered off the metal wall. The noise inside must have been shocking but still no-one appeared to give us a bollocking.

Then without the slightest bit of warning a figure came charging out like a bull with a hedgehog jammed up its arse. Looking back now, Fawlty was probably on nightshift and enjoying a well-earned kip when the bombing finally took its toll and woke him from his slumber. He louped over a high fence like it wasn't even there and chased us all over the place. Luckily we were all fit and able to stay far enough ahead of him. In truth, it was probably fear more than fitness that allowed us to outrun this madman who no doubt wished to tear off all our limbs.

The second incident came about after a few of us had gone for a wander out of Fintry and into the vicinity of some cottages near the farmlands. Out of the blue someone lobbed a stone onto one of the roofs and watched as it rattled and bounced down the slates.

'Hey, check this oot lads. Git yirselz a dockie an lob it on this raif – it maks a great sound.' And so we did. It was like déjà vu as we stood for ages, and launched rock after rock, totally fascinated by the sounds and not for one minute thinking we were actually doing anything wrong or damaging anything. Little did we know the owner had had enough of his roof being bombarded and raced out the back door of his house and into his car. It wasn't until we heard the scream of the engine revving and the wheels spinning on the gravel that we knew we were in trouble. Allan Wells would have struggled to keep up with us as we sprinted off down the road. As we went to hop a fence, Mac, who was at the back, nearly got flattened as the car did a handbrake turn and just missed him by a foot. This guy was seriously pissed off! He chased us over a ploughed field and wasn't that far behind as we scrambled up a fourteen-feet-high 'bendy' fence. The scene was one of sheer panic as bodies and limbs fought desperately to get over the wobbling mass of wire, and all the time psycho guy was gaining ground. The adrenaline was on full tilt as we all dropped to the ground in a tangled heap then sped off across the Powrie Park. Thankfully, our pursuer never attempted the fence and, without saying a word, he returned to his car.

We rested on a park bench and heaved in lungfuls of oxygen, relieved that the ordeal was over. Fifteen minutes later the ordeal was back on big time as psycho guy returned clutching two leads, which were straining to hold a pair of large Alsatians. We shot up and ran for our lives down a pathway and into the scheme and never stopped running till we reached our homes. That was *Chase-ays* on a major level which none of us ever wanted to repeat!

Another good pastime which could be dicey at times was *Backie Hopping*. This involved picking a row of back gardens and trying to run through them from one end to another. The best fun was had when it was dark, you were mobbed up and the gardens had loads of high fences and hedges to negotiate. I remember mates who were nearly decapitated when their necks hit a greenie line and others who were fortunate not to be halved in two when they ran into waist high wire fences. They received no sympathy, only howls of laughter, marks out of ten then told to 'git up aff thir erses an stop girnin like wee poofters!'

Playing *Cribby* was another very popular game and not nearly as dangerous as it is today. The streets were a lot quieter with far fewer cars on them so there was plenty space to play safely. Crib is the word we use in Dundee for kerb and the object of the game was to throw a ball across the road and try to make it rebound off the cribby. There were all sorts of points scored for different throws and catches and players could advance onto the white line in the middle of the road for bonus throws.

Tig was one of the games mentioned earlier where you'd run after someone and have to tig them. It had a few variations to it but none more controversial than *Shit-On-A-Stick Tig*! This was the daddy of all the extreme sports we played. The rules were simple – you found a stick, dipped it in a big dod o dog shite, then tried to touch your friends with it. There was no choosing of who was out at this one. The game just seemed to materialise when someone decided to poke a stick in a lump of keech and threatened to daub it on your clothes. However, once you'd tigged someone and smeared fresh Labrador shite all over their new Harrington jacket or ice-blue Sta-prest trousers, you didn't politely hand them the stick so they could get you back. No, you launched the stick onto a roof or up a tree then run like hell coz they were going to be slightly annoyed and want to smear some shite back on you or alternatively, rap your pus!

Playing *Cairds* (cards) was a seasonal thing played mostly by boys. Usually at the beginning of the new football season, cards were sold in packets and contained pictures of the latest players plus team photos and badges. I'm sure you got six in each packet and with these came a piece of brittle pink chewing gum, which lost its flavour after about ten seconds. Initially, you bought them to collect the whole set but very quickly realised this would set you back about a million quid! The companies who made them weren't daft and marketed them so top players like Kenny Dalglish were available in very limited numbers. What you ended up with was about three hundred doublers of Hugh Sproat, Drew Jarvie, Gregor Stevens, etc. You'd take a big wad of these cards to school and sometimes swap doublers.

'Lit is see wut yiv got there?' The person would then go through the pile and you'd reply for the next ten minutes with 'got, got, got, got' until finally a rarity would appear and you'd do a swap deal. You also got a 'checkie' or checklist to mark off what cards you had. Most boys increased their collection by playing games with them where you could win them. Some of the more popular ones were *Knock the Standy-upper Doon* or *Landy On*. In the first game, a card was stood upright against a cribby or a wall and each of you took it in turns to skiffy a card and try and knock it down. Whoever achieved this would then collect the whole pile of cards which had missed.

Landy On was similar except this time a card was laid on the ground and the object was to land a skiffyed card on or partly onto it. Occasionally, some lads would get fed up of playing cards and have a 'scrammy'. The word would go round the school playground like wildfire that 'sumdee wiz gittin rid o thir caird collection' and hordes would gather for the melee. This was a great opportunity to maybe get a rare card, especially if the boy had a good collection. The Panini stickers and albums were also on the go in the '70s but you could only use them for swapping, plus you didn't get a piece of brittle chewing gum in the packet.

Scubby Queen was a mildly barbaric game we were intro- duced to at High School and was played with a pack of cards and a fresh pair of knuckles. The rules are sketchy now but the end result was whoever lost would get the whole pack skimmed over their knuckles to the amount it said on the card. If you lost two or three games in a row the pain became unbearable as the deck thrashed over the already open and weeping knuckles.

Knifie was another dodgy and dangerous game for the obvious reason – it was played with a knife! Getting caught playing this nowadays would see you shipped off to a Young Offenders Institution for a six-month stretch for 'possession'. For us, carrying a knife was completely innocent and was used for the sole purpose of the game. Then it was returned to the house without a malicious thought ever entering our minds. This game also had a couple of variations to it. The simple version had you and a friend stand facing each other at arm's length with your feet slightly apart. The first person would throw the knife and try and stick it in the ground a few inches to the outside of their opponent's foot. He or she would then move their foot out to the knife, pick it up then do the same until you were both nearly in full leg splits. The winner was the person who didn't fall over and was able to pick the knife up. It was an excellent game for improving suppleness and balance and no doubt spawned gymnastic careers for hundreds of scheme kids. It's a real shame it never reached Olympic status.

The other version was much more interesting and daring and was played on a rope swing hanging from a tree. The first competitor would take a swing then try and stick the knife into the ground. The next person had to retrieve it then do the same. Very soon everyone became experts at throwing knives and the agility required to then pick them up intensified greatly. It wasn't uncommon to see someone hanging on with just their big toe and stretching way beyond the natural length of their body to grab the chib.

WUTZ THE GEMME?

Kick The Can was another personal favourite of mine and was very popular in the scheme streets back in the '70s. It was kind of like an intellectual version of *Hide and Seek* with similar rules. All you needed was a can and the idea was someone was out and would have to look for the others. The game started when someone took a runny and booted the can as far as they could then everybody took to their heels to find a hidey-hole. The one who was out had to retrieve the can then take it back to base and tap it on the ground as they counted up to fifty or whatever. They then left the can standing upright and went to look for the others. If they spotted a body they ran back and tapped the can saying 'so-and-so was caught'. The spotted then had to sit and wait at base while the others were also caught. The game had a wee twist though. If someone could return to base unnoticed and kick the can, everyone was free to take off again – all rather demoralising for the person who was out!

It would be impossible to play the game these days as the cans are all made of ultra-light aluminium. Back in the '70s a can *was* a *can* and made of proper can stuff like heavy tin! Once a can was gubbed and out of commission you simply had a rake in a bin and found another. The best ones were the large dog food cans – it was like toeing an old oil drum and gave you ample time to hide.

The girls had numerous games of their own as well as joining in with some of those mentioned above. They used to fill the school playground with games of *Elastics* and *Skipping Ropes* which were usually accompanied by little songs and rhymes. As mentioned previously, the cool thing for us boys to do was run through all these games snapping the elastics and tangling the ropes up – a great way to gain favour with the girls! Some became expert jugglers when playing

Doublers where they would bounce two or sometimes three balls off a wall while singing songs and performing intricate little manoeuvres. I remember the craze when *Hula-hoops* came out (not the crisp variety!) and you'd see girls shakin thir erses and twirling these plastic rings up and down their bodies, round their necks, arms and ears and everything else – it was amazing to watch!

Playing with *Clackers* was another phenomenon which many girls embraced during the 1970s and also injured many in the process. They were made up of two plastic balls connected by a piece of nylon cord and the girls would hold them in the middle and clatter these balls together at frightening speeds causing them to make a 'clacking' noise, whatever the hell that was. Someone must have gone to Argentina on holiday and saw ranchers use bolas to bring down cattle then thought, 'What a perfect toy to market for girls in Britain!' They were bloody lethal! Any part of the body caught in their path when in full 'clack' was going to experience a healthy dose of pain.

On a much lighter note and probably the next hobby they embarked on after suffering 'clacker clatter' was swapping *Scraps*. Girls would knock their mither's Catherine Cookson novels and fill each page with pictures of little fat-faced cherubs lying in clouds or pictures of kittens or vases, in fact all sorts of girly tosh and either show off these collections or swap one of these ugly cherubs for an even uglier cherub. For boys who didn't mind getting a good kick in the shins, a very tough and macho thing to do was grab a girl's book and turn it upside down so the scraps fell out and blew all over the shop.

As far as games go, you could probably fill a book on its own with all the various ones we played but there's one – in my view, the best – which I've saved for last. Playing *Marbles* or, as we called it in Dundee, 'marries', back then was like playing with an Xbox nowadays – only better! This was another of the seasonal games and each summer you'd see pairs or groups of kids all over the playground or in the streets in deep concentration, taking aim and trying to win their opponent's marbles by striking them. We were simply carrying on a great tradition from the generation or two before us. As I recall, there were a few different games you could play and rules and individual marbles' values were commonly known although in certain circumstances, up for debate.

Shops sold packets of marbles but I don't ever remember actually buying any. You'd find a few or get a few from a mate and that was you ready to get in about some matches. Without sounding like a bampot, I must have been fairly good at the game because I ended up with two large biscuit tins full of them (both of which are still in my mum and dad's loft!). At the bottom end of the marble 'pecking order' was the small, one-coloured basic model. This was a one-hit win if playing against a similar marble. The whole process got very complicated though as there were so many different marbles and depending on who had what, the scoring had to be agreed before kick off. Next up from that was a similar one but with two colours, then there was the 'Frenchy' which I'm guessing was so called after the tricolour of the French flag. However, anything with three colours or more was called a Frenchy.

'Clear-eez' or clear marbles were fairly rare and much sought after. You also got 'Putty-zirz' which we mistakenly thought were made from putty but were probably made from wood. I remember being in Primary 4 or 5 and a glazier was in school repairing a broken window. When he took off for his dinner break, a couple of us ran our fingers along the putty and tried to make our own marbles. They ended up looking like warped eggs though and were soon lobbed onto the school roof. The new window probably ended up falling out and the glazier probably got his jotters for shoddy work-manship.

'Chinese-eez' were my favourite marbles of all. They were often a real mixture of colours but I'm not sure why they were given that name. Possibly the wavy streaks of contrasting colours made them look like Chinese writing? These were highly prized marbles and once won, didn't usually see the light of day again. Most marbles were also made in a bigger version but not in any great quantities so were harder to come by. The bog standard little ones also had another great use – they were perfect for firing from a catapult an pannin windeez in!

Steel-eez were most likely ball-bearings from machinery and not marbles at all but they came in all different sizes and were an integral part of any collection. To win a reasonable-sized steel-ee required a fair number of hits. On very rare occasions someone would acquire one the size of a tennis ball but this was minute compared to the one my mate turned up at my door with one day. Liv gave me the familiar Tarzan call which we used on approach to each other's door. I went out to see him struggling up Fintry Road with this massive 'marble' in his arms.

'Check *THIS* ane oot!'

'Wahr the fuck did yih git that? It looks like a cannon ba fae Mons Meg!'

'Eh, itz a belter is it? Mac knocked it oot a gairden. The only hing is, eh canna git it in mih pocket!' That was an under-statement if ever there was. The thing was huge and I still remember him taking it back out of our garden and dropping it on the pavement which left a dent like a bomb crater. To this day I still don't know where the hell it ended up. Edinburgh Castle would've taken it in a minute!

Most boys kept their marbles in their school shorts pockets and sometimes, if someone had had a good day at the office with a few wins, their pockets would be bulging to bursting point. The strain on the material was too much and from time to time a pocket would burst in the class and unload the precious cargo. The poor lad would usually end up a few marbles 'lighter' as any stray steel-eez or Chinese-eez were fair game and given a new home. Some of the games could turn into epics especially if it was say, a Frenchy taking on a twenty-hit steel-ee.

There were some occupational hazards which sometimes couldn't be avoided during a match, like an older pupil toeing your marble away into oblivion or a prized clear-ee rolling under one of Fintry Primary's mobile or annexe buildings. If it did go under the mobiles it was a goner. The wooden annexe building was different though and offered us the opportunity to go looking for it at night and occasionally find a few extras. There were a couple of known entry points where you could squeeze under the wooden spars and into the area below the school floor which was about four feet high and extended the whole length of the building. You had to be extremely careful as the ground was covered in broken glass. Even in good light it was a very eerie place and people used to say it was infested with rats. It certainly wasn't a place for going in alone and a few times some of us, full of boyish bravado, went in the dark which was really scary.

One time I was with a pal and attempted to go in under one of the wooden staircases. Unfortunately, the hole was nowhere near big enough and I got my head wedged tightly between the wooden spar and the ground. The problem was my ear was jammed solid on the spar and I was in danger of ripping it off so I began to panic like hell with all sorts of horrible thoughts going through my mind. My mate went to get help at my gran and granddad's house but no-one was in. That's when I *really* began to shit myself. 'The rat's ir gonna eat is!' The more I struggled the more helpless I felt until I finally managed to wriggle free. Granted, my head looked like a burst rugby ball but I was out, and the rats hadn't got me!

By far the biggest hazards for marble players were the cundies (drains). There was no worse sight than seeing a favourite Chinese-ee roll onto the cundie grating then plop into the filthy water. My own children find it hard to believe when I tell them there was no hesitating – the cundie lid was lifted off, the school shirt sleeve was rolled up and you lay on the ground stretching for all you were worth, faking about in the rancid sludge till you got your marble back! If you were really lucky you'd get your own one and a wee haul of others that had fallen into the sewage 'marble graveyard'. The obvious downside to this was the horrendous stench when you pulled your arm back out but it was soon remedied with a wee rub on the grass to get the worst of it off, then you cracked on with the game. Anti-bacterial handwash, surgical wipes, aloe vera and ying yang sterilizing soap my arse! Your hands would only get washed later that night if you remembered –which meant no chance! Sometimes we'd lift cundie covers in the street for the hell of it and see if there was any booty to be had which, admittedly, seems totally unthinkable nowadays.

13

THE BERRIES

Most Dundonians of a certain age and older will affectionately remember going to the berries each summer to earn some much needed extra income. For many folk, especially the working class masses living in the city's housing schemes, picking strawberries and raspberries for money was very much a necessity. I have vague memories of Whitfield when I was very young and going with my parents to pick rasps from the nearby fields but this was just nicking them for fun to make jam. The outskirts of Dundee had an abundance of berry fields but as the city expanded outwards, many of these fields were eventually swallowed up by the schemes.

Our family hadn't long moved to Fintry when my old man took me and Steff to pick berries in earnest. I say in earnest but the reality of it for me and Steff anyway, was one big pus aboot. The initial problem anyone had was trying to get on one of the many berry buses which came in from farms near and far to pick up the skeemeez. Dan Mathews was a coal merchant and lived in the cul-de-sac across the road from us but in the summer he ran a double-decker berry bus. The memories have faded through time but the one clear recollection I do have is the heaving throng of humanity jostling and shoving and trying to squeeze through the open back end of the old bus. The scene was one of utter bedlam. Me and Steff were just two irrelevant wee bairns in the middle of an anarchic melee. Suddenly, my old man received the nod from Dan – he'd been selected.

'Uhv got mih twa bairns wi' is an ah,' said my dad. Dan reluctantly waved us all on. The thing was bairns took up valuable space but some of the best nabblers (pickers) had a squad of whippersnappers with them so they all had to be squeezed on. Health and safety was non-existent. The 'three passengers standing' rule felt more like thirty-three with another thirty-three upstairs, and yet we always got there safely. I don't remember where Dan's bus went to that day or if me and Steff even picked a berry. We more likely went away wandering and threw stones at the cows and sheep or dared each other to touch the electric fences. My old man had picked berries as a youngster but his adult career began and ended that same day at Dan Mathews'. As this was the Dundee Fortnight holidays and he was lucky enough to be in full-time employment, he had no real desire to pick berries, even if it was for cash! The real reason was probably to blood me and Steff and prepare us for our own impending 'berries careers'.

I was very lucky to have Sean Devlin as a pal in my class at Fintry. His dad Dode and mum Wilma ran berry and tattie buses among other things and when I was about ten I began going to the berries fairly regularly with Sean. It was great because you didn't have to endure the mayhem of the selection process to get on the bus. There was a real community spirit on Dode's buses and I'm sure it was the same on all the other scheme buses. Most people came from Fintry and knew each other so there was always a good craic going on. It was quite rare to go to another scheme and get on one of their buses as the old youth gang ties ran deep and outsiders were not particularly welcome. Some buses did, however, have various pick-up points and went into a few different schemes which had the potential to cause a rammy between rival gang factions.

Within Fintry itself you got to know who was running buses and where to congregate. It was comical sometimes when large numbers turned up for a bus and were turned away only to then head for the nearest alternative like a touring lynch mob. If you were still wandering about at 7.45am, it's fair to say you'd be unemployed for that day and it was a case of try again tomorrow. When I got a little older I managed to secure a job as a delivery boy for the morning papers but when the berry season came I wouldn't have been able to finish the round in time to get on a bus. In stepped the old man to take on the mantle of 'aaldist paper boy in Fintry' and cover for me. I can still remember standing on the street corners in among the throng of bodies waiting for the bus and seeing him pass on his bike with the luminous orange delivery bag. It did raise a few eyebrows and one or two comments like, 'Check oot the aald fart daein the papers!' and, 'Times must be hard fir the boy wen eez takkin joabs aff the bairns!' In truth, he wasn't that old at the time but I suppose it was quite bizarre to see an adult doing the papers. I didn't have the heart to tell people it was my old man but when I look back now, I'm so proud of him for doing that just so that I could get to the berries. I think he's still awaiting payment as well!

Dode's bus though was *the* bus to be on and as soon as the 'seevin weekeez' (school holidays) began, you were counting the days down to when the berries started. Again, I'm not sure where the fields were that we went to but when you were young it felt like you were travelling to John o' Groats. Quite often there were far too many nabblers on them and it's a wonder most even made it out of Dundee, never mind

Arbuckle's, Kirriemuir, Forfar or Blairgowrie. They were real old heaps that were manky and reeked of fag smoke and sweat but they were fantastic. If I could hop on one now the familiar smell would take me right back. I remember us younger nabblers sitting and standing near the open entrance at the back of the old bus as it hurtled along, which it could only manage when it was going downhill. There was no risk assessment, no cotton wool fence to keep you from falling out, no-one telling you, 'You can't stand there!' It was just freedom of the finest kind. In today's obsessive ultra-safe society, the thought of letting ten-year-olds (and sometimes younger!) travel away out of town for a whole day *by themselves* seems preposterous. Parents would probably be jailed for neglecting them and their children put into care.

My mum used to make my pieces up the night before and they nearly always had meat paste spread on them. I actually loved the stuff and I could consider myself luckier than a mate who once took a half loaf of bread and put the rasps he was picking on, greenfly and all! My rations were completed with a bag of crisps, a biscuit and a bottle of scoot (lemonade). Every bottle of fizzy juice was referred to as 'lemonade' but in truth this was only the clear 'lemon' flavour. Favourites were Sun Joy, Pola Cola, American Cream Soda, Irn Bru, Red Kola, Pineappleade, in fact the list goes on and they were all good. For some reason they were all fizzy as hell, a lot more so than nowadays. It was like drinking rough sandpaper or broken glass but the burps were humungous.

On arrival at the field you picked up a luggie (small bucket) and a big black bucket or metal pail then were allocated a dreel (row) and as the straabs (strawberries) were first in the season, you placed your piecey bag at the start of the dreel. The straabs were back-breaking graft but, one good thing, the buckets filled up quicker. Most people will agree one of the worst things of all at the berries was hearing that first berry hit the bottom of that empty bucket. You were expected to 'pick yir dreel clean wi' nae husks left in the berries' and Dode was always there to see that it was done. He was a larger-than-life character with a roaring voice that had the dead kacking thir breeks. He didn't tolerate any nonsense and everyone was expected to do their shift but he could still laugh the loudest and enjoy the banter with his squad.

The rate of pay was at best crap and at worst slave labour. In my early days it wasn't uncommon to hear farmers paying one-and-a-half pence or two-pence a pound. Incredibly, the real nabblers, many of whom were women, could still earn a small fortune. This was, of course, tax-free money and a lot these adults were signing on the Broo and getting money from the Social as well. They'd worked bloody hard for it and they sure as hell were going to enjoy it without any meddling taxman taking his cut!

When the straabs were finished it was onto the rasps and the opportunity to make a good deal more dough. Your piecey bag was hung on the dreel post at the start then you'd tie your luggie around your waist with the famous 'orange string' and begin picking. Once full you would empty into your black bucket then repeat the process until the bucket was heaped. The good thing with the rasps was you were allowed to squash them down in the buckets which meant you crammed more weight in. This type of picking was for the jam market and some of the more devious pickers would hide a dockie (large stone) or two in the bucket to increase the weight. This was a dodgy game for if you were caught at the weighs you could be lobbed off the field and banned from coming back. The farmers weren't daft and knew what went on, but great if you got away with it. There's no doubt they were joeying the scales and ripping us off, so it worked both ways.

One of the other scams which I never quite understood was peeing in the bucket. The thought of one pish making a difference and earning a good few bob was ridiculous. You would've had to have a pish like an elephant to make any kind of money! In my opinion the pishing thing was a wee shout back from the working classes to the rich farmers saying, 'Git it right up yiz coz ehv jist pished in yir berries!' The irony was that WE were the ones buying most of the jam! I always wondered why it reeked and left an aftertaste of pish on your palate but it was still good.

Then there were always one or two individuals who took the skulduggery to extreme measures and shat in their buckets. Apart from the fact that this practice was decidedly gross you would have had to drop a brontosaurus-sized dump in your bucket to make any additional impact at the weighs. It was hardly going to increase your take home pay now was it?

Although I loved going to the berries, it did have a couple of drawbacks for me personally. I used to suffer terrible bouts of hay fever but I suppose I was in one of the worst possible environments. My eyes and nose just ran constantly and some days my face looked like it had been clubbed with a baseball bat. If that wasn't bad enough, there seemed to be an endless swarm of wasps looking to share the berries with you. I was, and still am, scared of them and hate them with a passion. Every so often one or two of these 'stripey gangsters' would appear and buzz around my luggie which sent me into involuntary spasms while the air turned blue with screaming rants directed at them. If I went to empty my luggie into my black bucket and they were there before me, I'd stand in the dreel and throw rocks at them which usually ended in my bucket being cowped over and the berries spilling out all over the earth. It was a major distraction and they drove me insane!

With the long, sun-filled days taking their toll most of us ended up with what was commonly known as a 'berry tan'. You had two beautifully bronzed arms and a golden brown colour on your face and neck but a pure white t-shirt shape underneath which looked dead cool! And you always knew a nabbler because their hands and forearms were scratched to hell from the rasp bushes. One of the strangest things was when you went to bed at night and closed your eyes. All you saw were berries and bushes. As if a whole day of them wasn't enough!

Some of the farms you went to were well switched on and used to have a van come around at dinnertime selling snacks, juice and cans of beer at slightly inflated prices. The temptation was too much for some and their hard-earned cash was handed over far too easily. After the familiar cry of 'BERRY UP' which signalled the end of the day, some lads partook in a spot of underground gambling, usually in the form of *Pitchy* or *Same or Diff*. Both games were played with coins either tossed against a wall where nearest won or thrown up in the air and heads or tails were called. In extreme cases, some guys lost their whole days' wage in a very short space of time which was just mental.

One of the most soul-destroying episodes of berry picking was having your berries nicked. The game was hard enough without some low-life dodgy bastard prowling the dreels and stealing your buckets or punnets. It happened to me once and it was crushing. These sneak thieves took a real chance though for if caught they would have been dealt with by street retribution and smashed black and blue.

Most of the days, hard as they were, were filled with

humour and banter and it was great for us younger nabblers to listen to some of the 'adult talk'. Added to that, someone always had a tranny (transistor radio) placed on a post pumping out the latest sounds to take folks' minds off the graft. Berry fights would sometimes kick off when someone was bored and decided to launch a handful of raspberry sludge into the back of some unfortunate's head. Because of the height of the bushes it was possible to throw a pile of berries and clobber someone a few dreels away and get someone else the blame, which invariably ended up in a riot. When you think back now and see the abominable price of berries in supermarkets, we were lobbing fivers and tenners away at an alarming rate – just for a laugh! Twice I was thrown off a field for having a berry fight and twice it was with the same mate – Geordie. The first time we were having a carry on in a field away to the north-east of Dundee when we were told to 'get tae fuck!' by some huge teuchter.

'Ach up *him*, wull jist wak hame. It canna be far.' We didn't know where the hell we were at the time and just picked a direction and began walking through fields. At one point I attempted to vault a barbed-wire fence which tore my hand open and the landing saw me stumble and roll down a steep embankment and into a thick clump of jaggy nettles. Geordie thought this was hilarious, which it probably was, but not for me. I was floundering around, desperately looking for doakin (dock) leaves to soothe the stinging pain on my bare skin. It was only by sheer chance that we spotted the old Dundee to Aberdeen road and got our bearings. The fact we were both only primary school age didn't faze us at all, it was just a big laugh and a bit of an adventure.

The second episode unfolded just as the first had but this time we were even further away, somewhere near Newtyle.

THE BERRIES

It was mid-afternoon when we received our marching orders and we thought we had nothing more than a short and casual dander back to Fintry. It was in fact over ten miles and we had long since scoffed what meagre provisions and juice we had. The sensible thing would have been to accept the telling off and go and sit on the bus but we knew better. We must have been walking for a couple of hours when we heard the familiar roar of an engine and turned to see the berry bus hurtling past us.

'YIH BASTIRDZ!' we shouted, choking on the thick exhaust fumes while giving it the 'V' signs. 'STICK YIR BERRIES RIGHT UP YIR ARSE!' A minute later it was out of sight.

'Wahr the hell ir wih anyweh?'

'How do eh ken?'

'How far dih yih think it is tih Fintry?'

'Fuck knows!'

'Itz gonna tak aboot three days tih git hame. Meh mither's gonna murder is!'

'So's mine!'

It was an era of complete innocence and we eventually got a lift from some saviour after deciding to stick out our thumbs and 'hitch'. I can't remember if I got clattered from my mum but I'm pretty certain I wouldn't have divulged any information on why I arrived home so late.

Most of the schemes back then still had the remnants of berry farms in close proximity and they were always an option if you didn't get on a bus or just fancied making some dough nearer to home. The closest rasp fields to us were at the north end of the scheme run by a farmer called Tam Waite. They were handy if you just fancied doing some picking to make a few bob then buggering off back home. And because they were so near they were also perfect for nicking so your mum could make a pot of jam. When your mum was making it, the smell used to waft through the whole house and was absolutely mouth-watering, much better than the 'bought' jam.

Other popular farms within marching distance were Bentley's and Whitewall's although walking long distances when we were young was never an issue. I personally only went to Bentley's on a handful of occasions for the simple reason it was situated to the north of the neighbouring Kirkton scheme and there was a good chance you could get 'pulled up' and pasted from some of the Young Huns gang.

Witewahz, as we called it, sat roughly in between the two schemes but was a fair hike, again in a northerly direction. When the strawberries were beginning to get ripe a few of us would make the annual pilgrimage either by foot or on our bikes up an old dirt track which we called the 'Donkey Road'. I'm not sure if this was a name that had been passed down through the years or someone had simply come up with. It is still there today, and rises steeply uphill behind the new scheme of Emmock Woods where it deposits you out onto the Emmock Road. The farm lay about a quarter of a mile from there and without any thought for privacy we'd troop down and chap the farmer's door to ask, 'Wenz yir berries startin?'

Going into farmyards was always a highly risky business as there always seemed to be three or four rabid Collie dogs who ate skinny little scheme laddies in between their main meals. You learn from a very young age that the age-old call from the dogs' owner of, 'Dinna worry son, thull no touch yih!' is a big load of rubbish. What they really mean is, 'Dinna look Zoltan in the ehz, dinna pit a hand oot tih clap it, an dinna mak any sudden or jerky movements coz the doag'll rip yir limbs aff an strip thum bare then cha yir bahz tih a pulp!'

THE BERRIES

If the farmer or his wife *didn't* appear you were right in the shit because there was no-one to call Zoltan off once he started devouring you. In the main it was a great adventure and if you were lucky and got a 'start date' for the berries then the return journey was a delight, especially if you pedalled back down the Donkey Road. Getting torn to shreds by Zoltan and his disciples was considered a doddle compared to negotiating the white-knuckle descent of that hellish rocky surface.

14

SKEEM CUISINE AN SWEETIE CULCHIR!

With family finances run on a tight budget none of us had the luxury of our mums asking, 'Wut wid yih like fir tea the night?' No, the food was made and put down to you and if you didn't like it then you starved. This uncompromising situation didn't fair well with me at all as I was a complete fusspot when it came to eating, which caused many a riot between my parents and me.

The term 'tea' was and still is used in the schemes to describe your main evening meal. However this caused some confusion if you were maybe lucky enough to have the same meal in a more affluent part of the city:

'Good evening young man, what would you like for dinner?'

'Oh no, eh couldna eat anither dennir as well pal, ehv ariddee hud timahta soup an three dippy-ins. Nah, ehl jist stick wi' the tea an hae peh, chips an beans or sumhin!'

Dinner for us was served at dinnertime but these 'other folk' had lunch at dinnertime then dinner at teatime. I've never had lunch in my life! The only common ground where everyone was in agreement was breakfast but then it all went pear-shaped again when someone came up with the breakfast/lunch combo – 'brunch'. What the hell is brunch?

Anyway, as I recall, the fundamental ingredient of most teas back then was chips. They were the primary and most important part of the meal and everything else was built around them. Every kitchen was graced with a chip pan and after the potatoes were peeled they were cut into 'chip' shapes then bunged into the pan where they were cooked in boiling hot fat. These were *real* chips, chunky and manly, not like the effeminate little *French Fries* that plague our society nowadays. After use, the fat was allowed to solidify in the pan until the following evening when it would be called into action again. The longer this process lasted (sometimes months!) the more black crumbs of burnt fat gathered and I used to spend ages methodically picking them off my chips.

'Mum, thirz "buts" on these chips!'

'Ehl "buts on the chips" yih! Jist git bliddee eatin thum or ehl kick yir *butt* an yull be goin oot tih play nae futba lad!'

On the creativity side, opportunities were very limited and your menu for the week would run something like:

Monday – Ravioli and chips
Tuesday – Fish fingers, beans and chips
Wednesday – Potted Hoch, spaghetti and chips
Thursday – Beans on toast
Friday – Spam and chips
Saturday – Lorne sausage and chips
Sunday – Mince and tatties

This menu however, could change at the drop of a hat with certain items being deleted due to a lack of funds. When my mum was flush she'd sometimes splash out on a few slices of polony. The one piece of food I could never get my head around was the delicacy of cold meat with the boiled egg in the middle. Who the hell come up with that combination? And how the hell did they get the chickens to lay the eggs accurately in the middle of the cold meat? Another of life's wee mysteries!

Without trying to sensationalize things and plead too much poverty, food such as steak, salmon and chicken were extreme rarities and never reached most kitchen tables. Every so often we *would* get a wee treat and that was always a visit to the chipper (chip shop). In Fintry we were spoilt for choice and had the Blue Lagoon, Wallace's and The Fry Fayre and at weekends the queues were out the doors. There was no KFC, McDonald's or Pizza Hut and very few Indian or Chinese places. The culture has changed so much in a relatively short space of time. The first real takeaway (apart that is from the Chinese and Indian) I remember opening in Dundee was The Wimpy in the Murraygait although we were hardly ever in it.

So many children now seem to indulge in takeaway food on a daily basis, especially during school hours, which is worrying. I'm not saying we didn't eat any rubbish, far from it, but it seems so readily available now. During all the running about and burning of calories you'd maybe nip back to the house and get a piece on jam or a piece on tomato sauce to tide you over. Another scheme delicacy was dipping sticks of rhubarb into a poke of sugar, which was great for the teeth! Sometimes you'd nick rhubarb from a patch in someone's garden and scoff it as you walked along the street. There was no poncing about with washing it; you just tore right in about it. For all we knew it could have been covered in cat pish but we never gave it a second thought.

Another favourite pastime which threw up 'free' fruit was plundering. Apple trees were the most common but there weren't many of those in the schemes. If there were any locally you soon got to know about them and you knew roughly when the fruit was ripe and ready to plunder around September/October time. This was carried out mostly under cover of darkness by a highly trained hit squad of three or four mates and was made all the more exciting if the people were actually in the house. You'd quietly infiltrate their backies then scale the tree and start knocking the fruit. In order to carry a load you simply tucked your jumper into your trousers and put the fruit 'doon yir duke' as we called it, which made you look like a lumpy, fat bastard. Occasionally, the whole cargo was lost which, after much hilarity up the tree, alerted the owner who would come flying out of their house to give you a good kick up the arse. Bodies would dive out of the tree and plunge to the ground then make good their escape by any means necessary.

One time a few of us were up a tree in Fintry when we got rumbled and the guy came tearing out his back door throwing sharpened stakes at us. The scene was hilarious as the four of us tried to scramble over a fence in the dark with these things whizzing past our heads, although I'm not sure we would have been laughing if one had hit us.

The best and most daring raids were carried out in daylight up on the 'posh' houses of the Kingsway. Some of these gardens even had pear and plum trees which was an added bonus. Following a successful sortie we'd head back home trying to eat the whole pile of loot. The novelty soon wore off after two or three pieces and you'd end up throwing the fruit at people or parked cars or each other.

Like I said, you got to know where trees were and one location we'd visit every year was a field to the north of the city. It was commonly known as 'The Three Rows' for the simple reason it had three rows of plum trees. The raids up there had to be swift and decisive due to the fact the farmer's house sat at the top of the field and he'd come out with a large, man-eating Alsatian!

That then was the free cuisine but we did buy food as well, usually in the form of sweets and crisps. Anybody who grew up in that same era will recall the sweets being a lot bigger back then. Some folk will argue that because we were smaller the sweets simply looked bigger but I strongly disagree. We are being ripped off now and in some cases paying for a wrapper full of air where you end up saying to yourself, 'Ehm shair thirz a sweetie in here sumwahr!' Take Wagon Wheels for instance. They were so-called because they actually *were* the size of wagon wheels! Nowadays they're more like scooter wheels! Creme Eggs are more like spuggie's eggs now – they're bloody tiny! And Curly Wurlys should be renamed and shortened to just Wurlys as they're nowhere near long enough to curl! You'd also be hard pressed to find a Dainty big enough now to share with a mate.

We used to sometimes call sweeties 'swechies' and when you bought them you had to be quick off the mark and tell your mates, 'nae greeds', which basically meant 'no sharing'. If you were too slow and they got in 'greeds' before you, you had to 'cash them oot'. If there was a good few in the group this could be rather costly and leave you with next to bugger all. The sharing of a Dainty was always a contentious issue.

'Go an brack yir Dainty on the cribbee an gie is half.' You'd skelp it off the kerb but it never ever broke evenly.

'Ehl hae *that* half.'

'You kid awa an shite, thatz the *big* half! Thirz nae danger yir gittin that!'

'Och arite then, geez the wee half.' It wasn't until years later that you realised two halves of the same whole couldn't be different sizes.

SKEEM CUISINE AN SWEETIE CULCHIR!

A lot of sweets we used to get have disappeared from our shelves over the years such as Spangles and Kojak Lollies. Spangles were fruit flavoured boiled sweets in a packet and were nearly always included in a Selection Box at Christmas time. The makers must have over-produced them hoping they would fly off the shelves but they never really gained a big following and ended up as a forced extra in the Selection Boxes. They were always left till last and weren't eaten until April by which time you were getting desperate for a sweet. Just when you thought things couldn't get any worse someone would buy you a packet of another variety called 'Old English'. These were given as a punishment when you were bad because no-one in their right mind would have bought them to enjoy. They tasted like three-week-old rabbit shite!

Kojak Lollies on the other hand were blackcurrant flavoured lollipops made famous by Telly Savalas who played Detective Kojak in the popular TV series. Everyone would be sooking on them in the scheme and going around quoting his famous catchphrase, 'Who loves ya baby?'

Strange as it may seem, Victory V and Fisherman's Friend lozenges were fairly popular and sometimes we'd stuff a whole packet of them into our mouths which was like eating a handful of lit napalm. If you were really mental you'd drink a big glass of ice-cold water after you'd swallowed them which was disturbingly uncomfortable. Why? I don't have the foggiest!

During the summer months frozen Quenchy Cups were very popular. We called them 'Ice Tubs' and used to sook the juice from them until you were left with a block of flavourless ice. By that point your lips were numb and you had difficulty talking. One of the worst things about eating an Ice Tub was

145

pressing too hard on the bottom of the plastic cup which forced the fruity ice to pop out and land on the deck. This wasn't regarded as too big a deal and you simply gave it a wipe on your jumper and carried on sooking.

Ice lollies were hugely popular during the '70s with all sorts of flavours and varieties to choose from ranging from Draculas to Lolly Gobble Choc Bombs, Cider Barrels to Fabs and Zooms to Milk Maids and Mr Men lollies – the list was endless. Obviously, you could buy them at the shops but the most exciting option was hearing the crackly old tones from the Ice Cream van. It was like the Pied Piper coming into the scheme as bairns heckled their mums for a cone or a lolly.

'Mum, mum, kin eh git sumhin aff the icey?'

'No, uhm skint the now. Awa an hae a Rich Tea oot the brade bin.' Going into a mini huff sometimes worked and you knew when she went to get her purse the huff had worked. Its funny but I don't ever remember my old man supplying the dough for the icey, it always seemed to be the old lady who would scrape together the necessary coins.

'Here, awa an git sumhin then. Yir sister waants a Screwball an git twa Sliders fir me an yir dad.' On sunny days large queues would form and you hoped they hadn't sold out of the lolly you wanted. There was always a big cheer if some bairn had ordered a round of cones for a big family and didn't have enough hands to carry them all. A thick blob of ice cream would fall from the wafer and the bairn would go hurtling off, bawling into their house.

One of the bonuses from so much ice lolly consumption was the amount of lollypop sticks left lying on the ground. The streets were a lot messier in those days which suited us kids just fine. We'd collect five of these sticks and make a little triangular boomerang. They flew really well and used to explode when they hit anything. You simply gathered them together and built it up again – hours of fun!

I mentioned some of the lemonade earlier but by far my favourite was Cresta. In Fintry, they only sold it in the baker's next to R.S. McColl's and I remember the TV adverts with a polar bear saying, 'It's Frothy Man!' I liked Bazooka Joe Bubblegum or 'choonee' as we called it and I used to laugh when I read the tiny cartoon inside the wrapper but it wasn't the storyline which made me chuckle, it was the offers of bicycles or radios in exchange for ten billion wrappers! On top of that, you had to send them to America! You would have needed a cargo ship to shift that amount. Someone was definitely taking the piss.

I was quite partial to a Macaroon Bar on the odd occasion but one thing I could never understand was their popularity at football matches especially over on the West Coast. I just didn't get the connection between a big tough Glaswegian downing fourteen pints of Diamond Heavy then announcing to his mates, 'Ah could murder a Macaroon Bar by the way!' And yet, they sold by the bucket load. I often wondered where they originated from. Maybe it was named after a Scottish colony living in the African country of Cameroon? Maybe there's Cameroon Bars? Maybe thousands of African football fans were downing their Diamond Heavy before heading to the match and saying to their mates, 'Ah could murder a Cameroon Bar by the way!' obviously in an African accent though! Who knows?

Some of the other sweets we had in the '70s should have had a 'Danger to Health' warning attached to them. Mint Craknell tasted brilliant but it was like eating a mint flavoured pane of glass. Shards of sweetie would pierce your palate and rip it to shreds. Gobstoppers were another of the hazardous treats and had the capacity to get lodged in your windpipe and cut off your oxygen supply, whilst Space Dust had an altogether different effect and the little lumps of candy exploded like dynamite in your mouth, so naturally you stuffed the whole packet in!

Bags of crisps back then actually had some crisps in them! These days you open a packet to find ninety percent 'fresh air' inside – it's a total disgrace! Top brands at the time were KP, Tudor, Golden Wonder and Smiths. Without doubt the biggest and best value crisps on the market were Monster Munch. After a packet of these bad boys you were still eating pieces of them two hours later as they used to cling to your teeth. If I remember correctly some company launched a range of chocolate, lemon and raspberry (or strawberry) flavoured crisps but they were revolting and never caught on. These were out in the '70s and way before the chocolate crisps which were manufactured by some other company many years later and again, flopped.

The most extreme idea for crisps (since Twiglets) came possibly in the early '80s when someone produced the culinary classic 'hedgehog' flavour. To put it bluntly – they were terrible! They tasted more like shrew than hedgehog and I don't remember many people including them in their favourite snack lists.

Apart from the healthier side of the 'skeem cuisine' such as the beans on toast and Spam and chips square meals, the lasting legacy of eating from that decade is the mouth full of fillings most of us have from the sweets and juice we consumed. But it was worth every single sugar granule!

15

GOIN TIH GRAN'S AN LATER HOLIDAYS

I was very lucky to have both sets of grandparents around when I was growing up as a youngster. Even more unique was the fact I still had my great-grandparents alive (on my mum's side) and I remember the family going through to Linlithgow to visit them. For our generation, these were relatives who had fought and, thankfully, survived two World Wars.

Those great-grandparents Elizabeth and Jock were a couple of hardy souls and tough as old boots. They were also very warm, kind and loving human beings, given what they'd been through and had to endure, and these traits were passed onto my gran, mum and aunties alike. When you're very young you think to yourself, 'These people must be about two hundred years old!' Both lived into their nineties and their passing was my first encounter with death and realising the tearful emotions that go with it. My old man's grandparents had passed away long before I was born but he spoke about them with great affection. His mum had died when he was very young and my granddad later married Mina, the woman Steff and me knew as Grannie Robertson. She was an unbelievably kind-hearted woman who showed great love to both of us and all of our cousins. They lived in a tenement in Whitfield and when we went to visit, my gran would always spoil us with cakes and biscuits. The juice we were given though was usually ginger beer which I hated but drank anyway to be polite. It was like drinking liquid heartburn! Often, when we were about to leave, my gran would generously place a 10p piece into each of our hands which was a small fortune then to a bairn. At Christmas time we'd always get an envelope with a card and inside was a £1 note. You couldn't wait to get into town and spend it in the toy shop.

My memories of my granddad Robertson are happy ones although I remember him suffering through ill health near the end of his life. One time he nearly killed himself when he fell asleep smoking in bed and set it and himself on fire. He was badly burned but luckily he survived. He had served in the Second World War in the Royal Artillery, seeing action in North Africa and Palestine, then was transferred to the Argyll and Sutherland Highlanders as the Allies pushed into Italy. Although I was young at the time, I remember getting the phone call from my gran who asked if the old man was in and could she speak to him. I knew right away from the tremor in her voice that something was wrong. When I said he wasn't in and neither was mum she said, 'Tell uhm yir granddad's passed awa son.' I could hear her crying before she hung up. It was horrendous and all I could think of was how to break the news to my dad. It was a very sad time indeed and it took me a long time to deal with emotionally.

As I've mentioned earlier, my gran and granda Clark lived in Findcastle Place directly across from Fintry Primary School and there were times when I was there more than my own house. It's fair to say I loved going there and Steff and I were spoilt rotten. My gran (Betty) was one of four sisters and each of them was in contention for the 'kindest woman in the world' title. She had served in the Wrens during WWII and was a real grafter in civvy life, just like that whole generation.

My granddad (Nobby) had faked his age to join the Black Watch for the war effort. Like many of his fellow comrades they were mere boys when they marched into battle in 1942 at El Alamein in North Africa to fight Rommel's crack German forces. He used to relate his experiences as a stretcher bearer and recalled with tears in his eyes how, during that first hellish battle, his best friend and him were forced to take cover in a bomb crater as the German artillery laid down an incredible and frightening box barrage. He could only watch in horror as his buddy was torn apart in front of his eyes by a piece of shrapnel, killing him instantly.

Among all these tales of harrowing sadness were ones of complete hilarity, shock and amazement like the one he told of when his regiment were in Africa and they were using donkeys to transport gear. One of these beasts kept standing on his mate's feet and eventually he just turned around and cracked the donkey right in the pus and decked the poor thing.

In Sicily with the Black Watch, having just come through a bitter and fiercely fought campaign in North Africa and having lost many good pals, he had to listen as American soldiers arrived fresh to the fray on some beach and proclaimed in a typically arrogant Yank fashion, 'Don't worry Jock, we're here to finish the war for you boys!'

As Nobby remembered with a broad smile, 'He got eez pus cracked immediately then it wiz a battle royale as the kilties set aboot thum an pasted thum on that beach. The nivir went braggin again!'

From his time in Sicily he told me another story which was totally genuine. In fact, everything he told me about the War was genuine – I knew from the emotions he displayed when telling them. Him and a mate had got in tow with two local Sicilian ladies and were getting on handsomely, so much so

151

that having met their families they were offered the chance to desert and settle there. The families, however, had Mafia ties which scared the living daylights from my granddad. He admitted it was tempting and his mate was all for it but the loyalty to his mates and those who had already fallen was just too strong and they sensibly abandoned their floozies.

He also told how he and seven of his mates were asked by the British Army if they'd like to volunteer to go to Burma and fight the Japanese. If he'd decided otherwise I may not have been writing this book here today. He opted to take his chances fighting the Germans whilst the seven who went east sadly never came back.

Nobby was a tough and hardened man who had boxed in the booths as well as some unorganised bouts in the street. He didn't suffer fools and woebetide anyone who tried to take the piss out of him. Some of his employers felt the full weight of both his knuckles when trying it on. These were the days when, as he constructively put it, 'Yih kid crack a boy in the pus in the moarnin an go an git anither joab in the efternane!' He also did the doors with his equally tough mate, Sammy. If we were having too much of a riot in my gran's, he only had to raise his voice and the nonsense stopped instantly. The other side of his character though was a gentle and friendly man who loved a good laugh.

During the summer when Wimbledon was on, the Clarks' backies was turned into a tennis court and the whole family as well as neighbours would indulge in a highly competitive tournament. The younger ones got to be ball boys or girls but this wasn't a simple 'run and pick the ball up at the net' job like Wimbledon. For a start there was no net, just an old greenie line sagging across the garden. Our job was to go and rake in the hedge for a missing ball or hop over the fence and into the rough, overgrown jungle which formed a no-man's land between the houses and the tenements. This area was one big adventure playground where you could get lost for days building dens and learning survival techniques and how to evade your gran when she shouted you in at night. I remember falling in a pile of broken glass there when I was really young and screaming as the blood poured out everywhere – there seemed to be loads of broken glass lying around back then!

It was also an ideal place for Bonfire Night as you weren't bothering anyone and there was always an endless supply of burnable fuel which had been dumped. These were the innocent Guy Fawkes nights when we were all young and hadn't yet developed any wayward braincells that were only programmed for 'mischief'.

Nobby, however, was a professional 'Mr Mischief' and one Bonfire Night he decided to have his own fireworks display at Findcastle Place. Apart from the standard Roman Candles and rockets being launched from empty milk bottles, the night didn't liven up until he lit a few Barking Doggies. These little accordion shaped fireworks were very unpredictable and used to bang and jump all over the garden as if chasing you around, which was great. Not so great though was when he lit a thunderflash which he'd 'acquired' from the TA. The thing exploded and nearly took out half of Fintry and parts of Linlathen. My gran went mental at him but we thought it was brilliant and wanted more.

My gran was a bit of a soft touch and it was very easy to pull a 'sickie' and get off school. All you had to do was put on the dying swan act and add in a few groans and sighs and a bit of, 'Gran ehm no feelin well at ah.'

'Och mih wee lamb, yir lookin a but peely-wahly there. Jist leh up on the couch there an ehl git a blanket fir yih. Ir yih waantin the TV on as well or ir yih jist waantin tih hae a wee sleep?'

As soon as the blanket was over you it was head down and time for a wee kip. Nearer dinner-time you'd tell her you were feeling slightly better but not well enough to go back to school. By early afternoon you'd made a remarkable recovery and were tucking into a plate of stovies and watching Crown Court on TV – brilliant!

On the subject of stovies I think both my gran and granddad made the best in the world as well as homemade soup. In fact, my diet for nearly the whole period of my school days consisted of those two meals plus Angel Delight and thousands of pieces on jam. Me and Steff were so grateful for the close proximity to the school of our grandparents' house, plus it saved my mum and dad a packet not having to fork out on too many school meals.

In their kitchen hung an old clothes horse from the roof which I always thought was a pretty mental scenario. Having washed and freshened all the clothes up they were then hung up to dry in amongst the pungent aromas of cooking mince, onions, stew and the like, which made them very fragrant!

Staying over was always great fun and I'd listen to all the colourful family stories while tucking in to a large feast. Apart from my mum I had two wonderful aunties, Liz and Alice, and two smashing uncles, Alex and John. Fintry was still being developed when my grandparents moved there from Wilkie's Lane on the Hawkhill around 1950. My uncle John got to know some of the workies very well, so much so that at the age of nine he decided he was going to give them a hand and drove one of the steam-rollers away!

My auntie Liz lived in Salford in Greater Manchester so I didn't see her much when I was growing up. The same was true for my uncle Alex whom I mentioned earlier was serving in the Scots Guards. We lost him in 1980 in tragic circumstances when he was knocked off his motorcycle by a car. It was a hellish and painful time and he's still missed as much as ever. He was a terrific character and I suppose my gran and granddad paid me the highest possible compliment when they said how much I reminded them of him in looks and in manner which was very humbling.

My gran was forty-one when she had my auntie Alice and with her being only three years older than me, she was more like a sister to me and Steff than an auntie. With a gap of thirteen years between Liz and Alice my gran must have been somewhat out of practice on the old mothering skills when one day she pushed Alice in her pram up to the shops to get some messages. She returned home with all her groceries but forgot one small item – my auntie!

'JESUS CHRIST! UHV LEFT THE BLIDDEE BAIRN!' she screamed and tore back up the road like a maniac. If she'd been timed I'm sure she would have set a never-to-be-beaten 800-metre world record. As Alice was older I looked up to her and if she had said, 'Go and jump in the River Tay,' I would have done it. This loyalty to her nearly had me frazzled one night when we were visiting. The adults were downstairs playing Scrabble while Alice, Steff and me were upstairs wondering what we could play at. The old electric bar heater was on in the room and Alice came up with a great idea to liven up the night. She said to me, 'Go an touch the rade-hot bar wi' this Kirby-grip an see wut happens.' So I did just that and it caused a spark.

'Go an dae it again, that wiz dead cool!' After about four or five goes there was this almighty *BANG* and the whole house was plunged into darkness. Steff and me started crying as the adults went into a panic downstairs wondering what had happened. That night I must have had an angel looking after me because I really should have been blown through the wall.

There's no doubt these were simpler times and my gran and granddad were of the generation who trusted people in the community and thought nothing of leaving their doors and windows open. One night, some sneaky scumbag climbed in their window then stupidly proceeded to batter the gas meter with a hammer, looking to nick all the ten bobs. So much for stealth! The noise woke my uncle John who crept through to my granddad to tell him there was someone downstairs. He quietly slipped his trousers on then flew down to confront the burglar. It was his lucky night as the back door was open and he took off. Nobby grabbed his big axe from the coal bunker and chased him over the backies screaming, 'EHL KILL YIH YA BASTIRD!' but he didn't have any shoes on or a belt on his trousers and they fell down – but it was no time for laughing. He returned to the house then jumped into his car and drove around for ages with the axe beside him. The low-life thief can thank his lucky stars that he wasn't caught that night because my raging granddad would have chopped him up without hesitation.

The majority of our summer holidays throughout the 1970s were spent with my gran and granddad Clark and auntie Alice. As my dad didn't have a car till the latter half of the decade, me and Steff usually travelled in my granddad's car and my old man and old lady went by bus. There always seemed to be a summer heatwave on and huge traffic jams whenever we travelled south which was very trying on the patience. One year in particular tried everyone to the limit when we made the journey in Nobby's tiny Hillman Imp. It was like five of us sitting in a phone box with wheels on it. My gran used to have tons of sweets for the journey and she must surely have been in the top three of Britain's litter louts as she lobbed everything out the car window.

One year we went down to the Norfolk Broads and the seven of us shared a chalet together which was situated on a canal. The whole area is a massive network of rivers and waterways so we kids were well warned of the possible dangers and to be careful. On our first day my old man took me to the local shop where we hired a fishing rod and some tackle and bought a big bag of maggots for bait. 'Wir gonna catch a whopper son!' The line was cast and we watched the float for ages willing it to disappear but soon got bored and just left it.

The weather though was magnificent and we watched in awe from our veranda as the big flashy boats sailed by.

'Right,' said my granddad, 'we'll hae some o that an ah. C'mon, wir gonna hire a boat an show they posh fowk we kid dae the sailin thing as well.' Our budget however, was nowhere near the Miami Vice big cruiser yachts. No, we were going to spend our day sailing the high seas of Norfolk like a bunch of tinkies on a Chinese Junk! The boat was a heap of shite. Nobby took the whole thing very seriously though and had insisted we boys should look the part on the waterways so we all bought sailor hats. Mine was a little Popeye number while Rear Admiral Clark and Chief Petty Officer Robertson both sported dashing denim caps. Nobby looked every bit the old sea dog like some tough character John Wayne would play whereas my old man just looked like a little effeminate.

The excitement reached fever pitch as our floating pile of junk chugged and spluttered away from its mooring and out into the open water. We were now real life sailors and were about to embark on a daring adventure, prepared to take on rough seas, cut-throat pirates and Spanish Armada cannons. My gran was not thinking along the same lines though and was totally pertified. She had a life jacket on and incredibly, she was tied onto the back of the boat for safety! The fact she couldn't swim was of little importance as she would have gone down with the boat anyway, had we been unfortunate enough to have an accident. My old man was filming our day out on his cine camera and I think my granddad thought it was for Hollywood the way he was holding the wheel. We all got a shot of steering under his watchful eye and shouts of, 'Keep ir steady there!'

We did have a couple of hilarious episodes during the day. The first was when we stopped for dinner and moored up beside all these fancy yachts. It was like pulling up in a clapped out old Austin Allegro and parking between Bentleys and Rolls-Royces outside The Dorchester in London's Mayfair. Once we unroped my gran we laid out the tartan blanket and prepared to have some dinner in the company of our posh neighbours. My granddad fired up his little gas camping cooker, then my gran did her bit and placed the humongous pot of mince she'd prepared in the chalet precariously on top.

There's probably no need to write what happened next but I will. The pot fell off and the mince spilled out and onto the grass. Without any drama Nobby nonchalantly scooped it back into the pot, rabbit shite, grass, fag ends and all and got it back cooking. With my ultra-fussy eating tendencies, there's no way I was putting that anywhere near my mouth and I told my mum so in no uncertain terms. Nobby was made of sterner stuff though and would hear none of it. He picked a few blades of grass out then slapped it onto the rolls. 'Here, git that doon yiz.' You daren't say no to him.

Following our eventful and slightly embarrassing dinner we were back cutting through the water and trying to forget what we'd just eaten. Some time later it became pretty clear that we were lost. Nobby pulled over and asked a man and wife who were fishing if they could point us in the right direction. After a lengthy 'head straight on here, turn left then right', etc, etc, we thanked them then chugged on our merry way. Ten minutes later we were back in their company being given directions once more. The fourth time it happened we were all hiding with only an arm visible to steer the boat! It was like a scene from a *Carry On* film.

Whilst on that holiday we visited Great Yarmouth and the nearby beach resort of Sea Palling where my life nearly ended. Before that the whole gang of us stopped at one of the little beach shops where my granddad ordered up cones for every-one. The first one he was giving to my wee sister and asked if she wanted sauce poured onto it. Her mouth was watering in anticipation as he handed it to her. She took one big lick before nearly gagging, then started crying. He'd mistakenly lashed tomato sauce all over it instead of raspberry ripple and ended up having to eat it himself!

The beach itself at Yarmouth was stunning and the waves that day were massive so we all donned our trunks and costumes and waded in for some fun. I was only in waist high when this wall of water swept me right off my feet and tumbled me around. I was swallowing water and struggling desperately for breath and just as I got my head above water, another huge wave crashed down on me. At that moment I thought I was done for – drowned in little over three feet of water! My only saving grace was that my dad had turned around just by chance and noticed that I wasn't there then frantically waded over and plucked me from a certain watery grave. It was too close a call and I sat on the beach bawling my eyes out for ages thinking about what might have been.

The boredom of the fishing seemed much more enticing after that but our big plans for landing a whopper had failed miserably. During the week disaster had struck when a bird had torn into the bag of bait, releasing hundreds of maggots onto the veranda. The place was crawling and the girls were cracking up. On the final day, I reeled in my last reel and bingo, there was a little silver fish wriggling about on the hook. I was so excited as I wound it in although I didn't know what I was going to do with it. I watched in horror as Nobby made my mind up for me without any consultation whatsoever. He unhooked the tiddler and tossed it back into the river. I was distraught. All week I'd waited for this defining moment in my fishing career and it was lost without so much as a 'well done son'. I went away crying to my old man who explained diplomatically to me that my catch, brilliant as it was, wouldn't have fed the whole family and it was better back in the water.

That night Nobby and my old man went out for the fatal 'couple o pints' to celebrate a great holiday. They got chatting to some Welsh anglers and the bevvy started flowing big time and no doubt they began talking like a couple of seasoned professionals. We were fast asleep in bed when all hell broke loose outside on the river. A speedboat was ripping back and forth with the occupants shouting and laughing and my mum and gran instantly thought Nobby and my old man had knocked a boat. It was a false alarm and they didn't arrive until ages later. Both of them were absolutely steaming and my dad fell in the bath as he was getting a round of the guns. My mum was trying to shout at him but she ended up bursting out laughing with her mum and dad at my old man's misfortune.

Both of them suffered greatly the next day and my dad admitted sitting on a bus all the way home to Dundee with a raging hangover which was not big or clever. Nobby was in a worse predicament and had a monstrous 450-mile drive.

They were to top this drunken display a couple of years later and scale new heights of inebriation when we all went on holiday to Devon. My old man had passed his driving test by then and we drove down to the southern end of England in a fairly new white Chrysler Alpine after he'd traded in his first car, a Vauxhall Viva. For most of that journey we had to endure a mysterious ghastly reek inside the car. The problem was solved when we arrived and he noticed one of vehicle's battery cells had dried up so bang went a few quid on a replacement.

The cottage where we were staying was located in the middle of nowhere and had a distinct feeling of being 'haunted'. Apart from Nobby and my old man, the rest of us were shit-scared to go upstairs on our own. One night I nearly gave my gran a heart attack when I stuck a rubber bat behind the curtain in her room. I had just got tucked into my own bed when I heard an almighty scream and knew instantly what it was. My granddad went off his rocker and was going to strangle me but, thankfully, he saw the funny side later.

On the last night, just like The Norfolk Broads previously, they decided to have a 'couple o pints' in a village pub, nothing mental as they both had a long, long drive home the following day. When they got back to the cottage they'd already had a good few and now had a taste for it but there was no drink left apart from two souvenir porcelain flagons of Scrumpy Cider which they'd bought to take home.

'Ken wut John, wull crack open ane o they jugs an jist hae a gless o this stuff, jist tih see wut itz like eh?'

SKEEM LIFE

'Ach yir right Nobby, one each uhl no herm wih.'

Two empty flagons later and they'd done it again only this time they were horizontal guttered. This stuff was the real McCoy! I think we left Devon in July and got home to Fintry near the end of September.

16

THE FINTRY CLUBBIE

The Fintry Community Centre or 'Clubbie' as it was affection-ately known in the scheme was the main hub and centre of activity for young folk and youths to meet as well as adults and pensioners for hobby groups. And it wasn't just Fintry people who attended with folk coming in from surrounding schemes such as Whitfield, Mill o' Mains, Linlathen and Mid Craigie. It had opened in the 1960s to provide some much-needed entertainment and hopefully get young people off the streets and channel their energies positively. JM was an early pioneer and along with his dedicated staff they gave up much of their own valuable time to ensure the young folk were catered for. Those who knew him personally and who had attended the Clubbie during his time there spoke very highly and warmly of him saying he was a 'wonderful man'. Under his guidance, dances were arranged and bands would play which helped create a real community spirit.

The 1960s however, heralded the beginning of a city-wide gang problem which rapidly escalated into a very serious issue. (This subject is covered far more extensively in my other book *Gangs of Dundee*.) The decade had given birth to the first of these, the notorious Kirkton Huns who were quickly fol-lowed by the Shimmy, Douglas Mafia, Fintry Shamrock and so on until all of the schemes were represented with the Lochee

Fleet, Beechie Mob, Young Mary Boys, Mid, HULA, Hulltoon Huns, Ardler Pak and Whitfield Shams. Apart from the Shimmy, each of them took to wearing 'colours' to identify themselves and this came in the form of knitted jumpers and cardigans. Often huge numbers would parade around in these gang uniforms looking to set about another gang and the problem grew to such alarming proportions that headlines about it were appearing frequently in the local papers. So much so that in 1972 it was reported that 'if the problem got any worse in Dundee's city centre, the authorities would be forced to use water cannons to disperse rival groups'.

Community leaders like those at the Clubbie (and all the other scheme Community Centres) had a massive challenge on their hands to try and divert young people away from the 'romance' of gang culture. These were dangerous times and moving around town was a very hazardous task indeed, especially for guys who had girlfriends from other schemes. If caught on another gang's turf, even if you weren't in a gang, the chances are you'd get your head kicked in. It was a crazy situation, often volatile and violent but one which was generally accepted as part and parcel of growing up in that environment. By the mid-1970s the original wave of gang activity had gone into rapid decline which wasn't a bad thing. There were a few different reasons for this but arguably the main one was the arrival of Northern Soul. The music had a huge underground following in places such as Wigan and Manchester and rapidly spread north into Edinburgh, Dundee and Aberdeen. The beats and melodies were infectious and addictive and the music gripped young folk like a pied piper. Some of the dancing performed by these 'Soul punters' was extraordinary and could sometimes get very competitive as guys tried to outdo each other with acrobatic moves and spins.

Pretty soon bus loads of guys and girls from hitherto rival schemes were making the journey south together to *the* place to be – *Wigan Casino*. Instead of kicking hell out of each other though, they were dancing, together as one big happy family.

At the Clubbie, huge queues would form on the Friday nights for the 12–14-year-olds club. This was the most popular one by far and people would take their vinyl records along to get the DJ to play. The DJ was usually one of the voluntary helpers and a friend of those he or she was playing the music for. Occasionally they would hold an open disco where we younger kids would be allowed in with the older ones which made you feel all grown up. The venue also boasted a full-size snooker table, pool tables, table tennis, darts and football in the Fintry Primary school gym hall as well as a tuck shop selling snacks.

One of the big events which was organised every summer by the Community Centre and was eagerly anticipated by scheme boys from near and far was the 'Fintry Fehvs' tournament. This was the annual five-a-side tournament and was open to teams from all over Dundee. The games were played on the school pitch and huge crowds used to gather to watch and cheer on their favourites. I remember one year in particular when a team arrived from Douglas, all of whom were known members of the Toddy gang. Instead of changing into football strips, they chose to play in the gear they had arrived in. They were all skinheads and wore Doc Marten boots, bleached jeans rolled up, braces and either Fred Perry or Ben Sherman shirts. It was all taken in good fun and gave the crowd a right laugh.

A good few of us had joined the 5–11-year-olds club and enjoyed playing the games more than anything. Music and fashion were way down the list of priorities. This all changed drastically at one Friday night disco in 1977 for one reason and one reason only – punk rock! As we stood in the queue waiting to pay our entrance money it became very apparent that something spectacular had literally happened overnight. Older kids we knew were now barely recognisable with ripped clothes, safety pins, chains, badges and spiked hair. The 'Spike' haircut had never been seen before and was an extreme transformation from the fashionable long hair many wore. The whole thing just reeked of rebellion and attitude thanks to the antics of a soon-to-be infamous band called the Sex Pistols. Personally, I wasn't aware of the punk explosion which was taking Britain by storm – until that night. I just stared at people and thought, 'Wut the hell's happened here?' The music was fast, aggressive, fresh and full of energy and loads of youths became punk rockers instantly. The dancing was even more bizarre as folk pogoed around like maniacs then did the dade-flee (dead fly) on the deck. The spitting culture never really gained much backing certainly in the Clubbie as gobbing on a mate's clothes would have earned you a good kicking.

As younger kids we wanted to emulate these older 'rebellious punks' and it wasn't long before we were trying to immitate their dress sense and attitude. I remember watching Sham 69 singing 'Hurry Up Harry' on Top of the Pops and thinking, 'That'll dae fir me!'

'Right mum, eh waant yih tih git yir sewing-machine oot an tak in ah mih troosers skin-tight so thir like shite-catchers. An wile yir at it, kin yih sew a load o zips on thum.'

'Wuddiya mean zips? Wahr aboot?'

'Jist ah ower really. Itz smart as anyhing!'

'Nah, uhm no daein it, yull look like a bliddee mink!' This was the cue to go in the huff and eventually the old dear would give in. Any trouser bottoms more than three inches wide were considered 'flares' and you'd get slagged up. Some were so tight that you had to wrestle around on your bedroom floor before managing to squeeze the heels through them. Getting them off was even more difficult. The tightness did cause a problem though when you were out playing as they didn't offer much mobility at all. Then of course you had to tear the gear up and splatter paint on them then add the badges, chains and safety pins. My old man hated the whole thing and used to say, 'Wut, dih yih hink yir a wee hard man or sumhin?'

When I asked my parents for a pair of ten-hole Doc Marten boots I was refused point blank. I did eventually get them though and the trousers were soon rolled up to reveal the whole boot – cool as hell! However, worse followed with my old man when I started buying records and playing them at full volume on the record player in my room. He'd be enjoying a nice peaceful tea after a shift in the jute mill when on would come Slaughter and the Dogs with 'Where Have All The Bootboys Gone?' He'd go off his trumpet and bawl up, 'Wull yih turn that shite aff, eh canna hear masel think in here!' I'd turn it down temporarily then gradually crank it back up to ear-splitting levels. It must have been a nightmare for him because whenever I bought a new single, the record player arm would be left over on 'repeat' and the song would belt out all evening. When the sweary stuff like 'Friggin' In The Riggin' by the Sex Pistols began hammering out he threatened to 'smash the hale collection!' It's funny but when I got older he admitted his father was the exact same and used to go off his head at him when he kept playing 'that bliddee YEAH, YEAH, YEAH, rubbish by The Beatles'. History was just repeating itself.

By the end of the '70s the music and fashion scene was

extremely varied and diverse and young people were following everything from Punk, Mod, Northern Soul, Ska, Heavy
Metal, Skinhead, Rockabilly and of course Pop. A few of us
would go down town to record shops like Chalmers and Joy,
I & N's, and Cathy McCabe's to buy our singles. We rarely
bought LPs because no-one had the money.

Like I said, the Clubbie discos were brilliant and you'd hand
your vinyl over to the DJs and wait for the first few familiar
notes then spring into action on the quickly-vacated dance-
floor. We had a right laugh at one of these when Mac appeared
with a freshly bleached pair of modern 'stretch' jeans. He must
have used undiluted Domestos to splatter over them because
they were honking. A few pogos into the first song, the strong
bleach took effect and began eating into the stretchy material,
causing them to literally fall apart. We were howling with
laughter as he had to head back up the road and change his
breeks.

The guys who spun the sounds were mostly Soul punters
and we'd have to wait ages for a pogo but if it wasn't for some
very special guys like Danny Feeney, John B, Podge, John L,
ex-Dundee United legend John Reilly, Alan W and others
volunteering and helping out, we would have had a very dull
community centre.

The guy who was at the helm though and made the place
tick (just as his predecessor JM had) was a man called Charlie
Morgan. Charlie did a magnificent job keeping us all in line
and making sure we had fun at the same time and he certainly
had his work cut out when the glue-sniffing epidemic caught
on. All of a sudden loads of young folk began spending their
pocket money on tubes of Evo-stik or Bostik and taking a one-
way ticket to the moon on a magic carpet, except sometimes
the carpet had a hole in it and they'd crash back to earth with a

BANG after a bad trip. Taking drugs was nothing new among the youth of the schemes but 'sneggin the gleg' (a term which came from 'Eggy' language) was something completely alien and uncharted. It wasn't something I ever thought about trying as I was too scared I wouldn't be in control and of what my old man would do if I went home tripping. On top of that I really enjoyed keeping fit and sniffing glue didn't fit the bill. Peer pressure was (and still is) a huge thing for young people and it took an enormous amount of willpower to say 'no'.

'Here, geeza pour, yiv got a hale tin there. Jist pit it in this crisp bag.'

'Geeza bla efter yih?'

'Eh arite, but yull hae tih wait tull uhm trippin oot ma pus, then yih kin hae a bla!'

'Eh nae baather but hurry up.'

'Getting a pour' was a share of the glue and a bla (blow) was an inhaled share of it. The term 'sniffing' wasn't strictly correct as the glue was taken in through the mouth via the neck of a bag. Some guys would take this to extremes and have a carrier bag with a large pour inside. It was a mental period with body's stotting about the schemes totally out of their nuts. At the berries some folk were actually picking and basing their wages on how many tubes of glue they added up to.

As well as the glue, people took to sniffing gas and lighter fuel which was equally as dangerous and you'd see these souls inhaling fumes from their sleeves or a rag. And then there were the 'free' drugs – the hallucinogenic magic mushrooms. Golfers struggled to play their shots on the fairways of Caird Park and Camperdown golf courses where the mushies seemed to grow in abundance, for fear of cracking some youth in the skull with their ball. Mind you, they probably wouldn't have felt it. One hundred of these little stems of dynamite boiled in a pot of tea could see you off to planet Jupiter for a good few hours.

Then of course there was the bevvy. In keeping with generations past and present, under-age drinking was rife. There were no fancy alcopops around at the time and a standard carry-out consisted of a bottle of Merrydown and two tins of Super Lager or Carlsberg. The latter two tasted like the liquid wrung from a wrestler's jockstrap – they were positively awful and enough to put people off drink for life. The fact that alcoholics have made them their favourite choice of beverage for years says it all. Youths however, weren't drinking it for its smooth and scintillating massage of the tastebuds. They were drinking it to get pished because it was as strong as hell! At the Clubbie, Charlie was always on the look out for those who had been indulging, basically for their own safety and if caught, they were usually ejected with a stern word in their lug (ear) to 'git yir arse up that road'. There was rarely any need for police or parental involvement because he knew what kids were like and that sometimes they were stupid and they respected him for that. It is no exaggeration to say that people such as Charlie and JM were without doubt hugely inspirational characters within our communities and I'm sure I speak for everyone when I say a massive 'THANK YOU' from a whole generation of scheme kids.

Following a comparatively quiet period, gang culture made an enormous comeback towards the end of the decade when a new breed of scheme warriors resumed old hostilities and replaced original members, many of whom had moved on, got married, started working, joined the army, etc. We attached ourselves in varying measures of loyalty to the 'Shams' and unwittingly terrorized the senior members of our community whilst attempting to fight for the honour and good name of Fintry. I was no scrapper and would throw bricks from the back of the pack while shouting the odd, 'Shams rule ya bass,' not that the opposition would have heard it as I was so far from the action, but it made me feel like I was lending my scrawny seven-stone bulk to the cause. As the gang uniforms returned, so the tribal boundaries were enforced. Suddenly, it wasn't safe to walk into other schemes unless you went mob-handed and the youth gangs ruled the streets once more.

17

FAE BUSINESSMAN TIH FREEZIN PALMS

Living in the Dundee skeemz in the 1970s had its fair share of the good and the bad in life but I've left some of my favourite memories till these final chapters. As I've said, our families didn't have much in the way of spare cash in the '70s so, with very limited spending powers, the onus was on us to go and make our own fun. And as well as that, we were always on the lookout for ways to make a few bob with little 'business' ventures. My wee mate Liv and I were constantly striving to make our way in the business world and one or other of our little schemes sometimes came up trumps.

All you needed was a brass neck and a bit of charm to go chapping doors and ask the occupiers a simple little question: 'Ho Missus, dih yih hae any aald empty liminade bottles yir no waantin?' This wasn't always received too well, especially if you'd disturbed the wifie from watching some drivel like *Crossroads* and you'd be told in no uncertain terms to 'bugger off oot mih gairden!' In the main though most folk would politely say, 'Nah sorry, no the day son,' and close their door. When this didn't happen and they went away up their loabee (hallway) you knew you were quids in, or more specifically 'pennies' in. With a penny back on each bottle the incentive was there to collect as many as possible and trade them back in

172

the shops for sweets. This gradually went up from a penny to two pence and then five pence.

One time, Liv and I were chapping the tenements in Fintry Mains when we hit a 'lemonade bottle Klondike'. When the wifie opened her door we gave it the usual, 'Any empty liminade bottles?' to which she replied, 'Oh, yir in luck lads, ehv jist pit a few oot tih the bins.' We followed her down to the bin recess excitedly, thinking that we may get five or six but nearly whooped with joy when she said, 'Here, thirz three kerrier bags fuhl o thum!' We'd hit the jackpot. 'C'mon, lit's git up tih the chipper an stuff wir pusses! Wiv got enough here fir twa 12s o chips, twa bottles o scoot an a load o sweeties as well,' and that's exactly what we did.

The ironic thing was that if my old lady sent me down to the shops to get a message and she asked me to take an empty lemonade bottle with me to get some money off, I hated it. Especially if there were two bottles in the carrier bag and they rattled together on the way to the shops. This was seen by some as minky and you'd try everything to avoid being spotted or 'accidentally' leave it in the house. It was bizarre.

Another good earner was wedding scrammy's or 'scrambles' as some people called them. With two churches in Fintry you had a double chance of there being a wedding on a Saturday. When there was one on, your main worry was too many people getting wind of it, thus lessening your chances of a good lift. Sometimes the older boys would appear which meant you'd be lucky to get a couple of coppers. The ragamuffin horde would wait, jockeying for position then explode into action when the handful of change came flying from the car window. Everyone went after the silver first before turning their attentions to the lesser denominations. Skint knees and elbows were just painful by-products in the quest to gather some coinage. There were the odd few weddings however when you'd spend ages waiting for all the boring churchy bits to finish then off you'd go, running after the cars, waiting for the shower of coins to fly out, only for them to take off without scrammying, to the uncharitable shout of, 'Ach, eh hope yih end up divorced yih stingy bastards!'

I touched on nicking berries from nearby fields earlier although that wasn't for financial gain and was merely done to boost the old lady's home made jam supply. There *was* dough, however, to be made in some of the other fields and anything in the vicinity of the scheme was fair game. Nicking tatties was probably the best way to make a good few bob. We genuinely believed we were doing no wrong as the farmer had a whole field full of them but with our sustained nightly raids I suppose it would have made a bit of a dent in his supply eventually. One field in particular was just across the Forfar Road and near to the Mill o' Mains housing scheme. Incidentally, there was a little wooden shop situated in between the two schemes which used to get a hell of a time from us. On the gable end inside they had all their tins stacked against the wall so we'd take turns to run and do a flying Bruce Lee kick at it, sending the tins everywhere. Then we'd take off howling with laughter ready for a later return when the shelves were re-stacked. It wasn't the most sensible thing to do! Even though the gang thing was on the go, Fintry youths generally got on with their neighbours and indeed, many of us were classmates at Linlathen High School and also friends. Some nights, the lower ends of the field were mobbed with 'tattie rustlers' but the location had one big drawback – it was wide open to the roads and therefore easily viewed by a passing panda car.

Everyone would be busy bent over and filling their carrier

bags when the cry would go up, 'Run fir it lads, here's the Fuzz!' If they were far enough away you'd leg it with the bags but mostly you had to leave them and scarper until the coast was clear and you could return. Time was money and the polis just got in the way. We'd go selling our booty round the nearby streets and a full carrier bag could fetch ten bob (50p). Some housewives would actually place orders if they'd missed out, which was great but you had to hope some dodgy mate hadn't stepped in and stolen the sale while you were off filling the bags.

In winter we'd arm ourselves with a spade and go chapping doors asking if people would like their paths cleared of snow. Again, on a good day, it could bring in a few bob but it was bloody hard graft, especially if they wanted the backies cleared as well!

Winter was a great time and the fun we had was endless. If there was a real sharp frost but no snow, we'd get buckets of water from whoever's house was nearest and pour it all over the pavement and wait for it to solidify. Soon enough we had a ready-made skating rink which didn't go down too well with passing grannies.

'Yih silly wee buggers!' they'd shout. 'Sumdeez gonna skite on thir erse an go ah thir length!'

'C'mon then, gie wiz ah a laugh grannie!' Youngsters these days are rarely afforded the same luxury as the Council path gritters are out pronto, spoiling the fun!

When it came to sledging we had a cracking slope called the 'Burnie Brae' down at Finlathen Park. The only problem with it was the amount of trees spread around the lower half of the slope and the raised areas where people would tee-off in the summer for the pitch and putt. My old man built Steff and me a sledge which we used for years. It was solid and heavy but went great in the icy conditions when the snow was hard packed. Two years in a row I nearly joined the fraternity of eunuchs when I flew off one of these platforms and hit a tree with my legs spread. My balls battered off the trunk then my forehead followed a split second later leaving me in a terrible quandary of what to hold first as I screamed in agony!

The Brae was fantastic and proved a real magnet for kids as soon as the first proper snowfall had landed. An army of scheme bairns would descend on the slope and pretty soon after it was turned into a polished ice run. Very few people had money for fancy plastic sledges and made do with just about anything that would slide. Old ironing boards worked a treat, as did baking trays, shovels and plastic baker's crates. One of the best sliding vehicles was a large piece of thick polythene. A few bodies would take off down the slope before a wild rabble leapt on to create a hurtling melee of flailing limbs. The folk whose houses faced onto the park must have totally hated the arrival of the sledging season. Their living room windows were easily reached with a snowball and were hammered relentlessly. The great thing was you never got caught because you simply took off down the brae and made good your escape. In fact, belting any window with a snowball was great fun and an excellent way of getting home quickly at night, running from an irate occupier.

Throwing snowballs at Linlathen High School was in a complete league of its own though. It didn't really matter if the weather was foul, we'd be let out at playtime which suited us just fine in winter. The last thing you'd be warned was, 'Now remember, no throwing snowballs!'

'Eh right! Litz git right in aboot it!' Huge squads would gather on the playing field and wait on one of the buses coming up the main Forfar Road. The bus stop was right outside the school and nearly always stopped to let a grannie on, probably on her way to enjoy a relaxing game of bingo or a trawl around Littlewoods store in the town looking at cardigans and frocks, followed by a cup of tea and a scone and a good gas with her pals. As soon as the driver stopped and opened the doors it was just total carnage! To be honest, it could be likened to hunting sheep – there was just no difficulty involved in locating and hitting a target. Even better was when the doors in the middle of the bus opened as well to let someone off. The poor driver and his passengers didn't stand a chance as volley after volley of white dynamite exploded in their faces. Again, it was another of those completely irresponsible things we did which we thought was hilarious at the time. Our fun was someone else's misery. Oh the shame!

18

UP TIH NAE GADE

On the subject of buses, I remember the old green double-deckers (just like the berry buses) and how packed they'd be. The conductor would have his work cut out trying to dish out the tickets with his little machine and making sure there were no sneaky-ons. All the smokers used to sit upstairs and the bus was always minging. They only had one entry and exit point at the rear which didn't have a door and if you were sat near the back in winter the bus was bloody freezing. Some of the cooler guys would leap off the bus as it approached their stop at speed, which was highly impressive. However, it could also make you look like a complete arse if you got it wrong and many did, breaking ankles and crashing onto the road or the pavey in a mangled heap. Everyone else thought it was side-splittingly funny though.

The move could also be made in reverse for boarding and my old man once made an utter dope of himself when attempting to 'coolly' get on a bus that was still moving. As it approached the end of Arthurstone Terrace it slowed down to take a sharp left up Albert Street where it was about to stop some 100 yards up the road. The successful mounting of the platform was all down to impeccable timing but as the old man had downed a few pints earlier his timing was out . . . quite a bit. He got the little jog bit right and his grabbing of the pole was spot on but the critical 'step up' part went disastrously and his foot slipped off. He held on for grim death while pedestrians and passengers alike watched him being dragged up to the stop. His winkle-pickers (shoes) were in tatters by the time the bus halted. So was his 'coolness'.

When we were young, climbing was one of the arts we mastered and this was utilised to full effect when playing on tree swings. Some of these things were massive and you took your life in your hands when playing on them. The most dangerous bit about it was you didn't know the condition of the rope and whether it would hold your weight. Loads of boys ended up with broken arms and legs when a dodgy rope snapped and slammed them into the deck. The higher you could climb, the better the swing you got and some were tremendous. Others you had to climb up a nearby tree and get a mate to throw the rope up, then you took off in an incredible pendulum arc. Depending on where the rope was tied on the branch, you occasionally had to count the number of 'safe swings' and when you had to get off before you'd slam into the trunk. Unfortunately, I found this out the hard way in spectacular fashion on a swing over the Burnie. The horror of swinging away up a steep embankment then accelerating rapidly downwards and realising the trunk is about to greet you, with all the comforting feeling of diving from the top chairy (board) into a concrete swimming pool, is slightly distressing! I hit the tree square on then slid down the muddy embankment and into the water. All judges awarded straight sixes then fell about laughing, while I just fell about in agony.

Undoubtedly, one of the most dangerous swings in the whole of Dundee was the one just up from the Longhaugh Hotel which swung out over the old quarry. The sheer cliff face dropped a few hundred feet below and was intimidating as hell. It was mostly bigger laddies who hung about there (pardon the pun!) and they were welcome to it. It was just mental! The seat of the swing was either a big knot or a piece of wood through a loop. The latter was slightly uncomfortable but better than the knot. However, when a few mates decided to get a 'hudgie on' (pile on), the pain became unbearable as your arse cheeks bore the extra weight. It felt like your legs were going to slice clean off. This action was also a recipe for disaster as you could all be swinging thirty feet above the Burnie when the rope snapped!

Although we played in and around the Burnie I don't remember doing much fishing in it. It maybe had something to do with some of the alleged chemicals that may have found their way into the water.

'Oh yih dancer, ehv got a bite!'

'C'mon then, git it reeled in.'

'Oh ho, here it is. C'mon, come tih daddy.'

'Wut the fuck is THAT? Itz got twa hades an three tails? Thirz sumhin no right!' I'm having a laugh of course but in saying that, I sometimes had a drink of the Burnie water and it never did me any harm. If someone had a rod or a 'throw-ay out line' we'd hop on a bus and go down to the Broughty Ferry harbour or over to Tayport and fish for flookies (flounders).

Most scheme boys' and girls' introduction to fishing though was buying one of those cheap little coloured nets fixed to a bamboo cane, taking an empty jar and heading for the nearest little stream or pond. The closest one I remember to Fintry was a very small stream which ran along the field (where we nicked the tatties) to the north of Mill o' Mains. It was more like a swamp than a stream but it did have a few tiddlers in it. These were the minnows we knew as sticklebacks and we'd fill our jar with water then put them in.

Strangely enough, at the time, we thought we were catching another species which we called 'rade (red) gubbers' but these were in fact the males whose bellies turned red during the spawning season. I caught one of these at another popular location in the small stream at Caird Park which ran from the Den o' Mains ponds and, amazingly, it lived for over a year, nine storeys up in a Whitfield multi in our fish tank.

The Cairdie was a great park to play in, especially round the double pond area and also in the derelict Mains Castle and nearby graveyard. The castle was an old home of the Graham clan dating back to the 1500s. I always remember this as there was a large scribed stone somewhere above the doorway on the huge outer wall and although the castle has since been refurbished and restored, the stone has sadly vanished. The place was a death trap which I suppose is why so many kids were attracted to it. The walls provided excellent challenges to test your climbing skills while the lower basement rooms tested your bottle. It was pitch black in them and eerie as hell and I personally never ventured too far into them. The graveyard or 'gravey' as we called it was situated across the stream and has some ancient headstones dating back to the 1600s. It was a great place for playing hide and seek but, sadly, this has been badly vandalised and totally neglected.

Although the park was a great adventure playground with some smashing conker trees thrown in, the place held a darker side which I'm not sure was myth or fact. As we were up there a lot we'd often come across a rather dishevelled man who seemed to be around the pond area a lot and, sometimes, milling about in the bushes. Occasionally there was a boy with him who was around the same age as us. Rightly or wrongly, he was commonly known by most as 'Dirty Jim'. Instinct told you to stay well clear of him and we always ran away when we saw him. This was way before anyone had ever heard of the word 'paedophile' and knew what it actually meant. Whether the guy was or wasn't is irrelevant but one thing is for sure – the gut feeling said that something wasn't right when he was around.

Sometimes I'd save my pocket money up and go to the Saturday Show at the Odeon cinema (now Déjà Vu Nightclub) across from the Wellgate. Going to the pictures was a real treat and those mornings were just one big riot. Mums would leave their bairns in there for a few hours while they went and did their shopping. It was like one big crèche without anyone actually looking after you. The ABC cinema ran a similar show as well but it was the Odeon I went to the majority of the time. We'd nearly always make a bee-line for the trick shop in St Andrews Street or the one in the Seagate and stock up with some ammo, mainly sneezing powder, itching powder and stink bombs. You'd wait till the lights dimmed before chucking the sneezing powder into the air or quietly pouring some itching powder down someone's neck. And the stink bombs? Well, they were self-explanatory! I still find these little 'jokes' hilarious as a grown adult! The place was in one big uproar until the serial began. At the interval youngsters would be encouraged up onto the stage to 'have a dance' before the main film came on. It was just bonkers but great fun.

The build up to Guy Fawkes Night was as keenly anticipated as Halloween. We'd go round the doors asking for any old salvage for our fire and sometimes make up a 'Guy' then ask, 'Penny fir the Guy?' It wasn't as profitable as guising but you could still earn a few coins for sweets. The wood would be stockpiled for the big night but if rival mobs got wind of where your stash was, they'd either knock it or set it on fire and you'd have to start again. Pocket money would be saved in advance to buy skweebs (fireworks) usually from the aforementioned trick shops. We knew fine well that they were dangerous but this was the one opportunity a year where a bairn could happily play with explosives. Were we responsible with them? Were we hell! Bangers were the most popular and were easily chucked about like little sticks of dynamite. Sometimes they'd be lit and placed into a friend's jacket pocket which set them into a right panic! Or we'd put them into a milk bottle and watch it explode. Some nutters took it way too far though and put lit bangers or small rockets through people's letterboxes which was unbelievably dangerous!

Of all the home made toys that we had to amuse ourselves with and create a little fun, the kite was by far the simplest to construct. All you needed was a long piece of string attached to an empty carrier bag and a good stiff breeze for hours of happy flying. You could even have designs on your kite to add a touch of colour and artistic flair.

'Ho, meh kite's smarter than yours. Ehv got a rade Wullie Low's motif emblazoned right across mine!'

'Awa yih daftie! Mine's might be a but plehn but at least itz stull on. Your fancy pish huz jist blew aff yih prick! Yull hae tih git a new ane!'

The search for old pram wheels was still fairly popular during the 1970s although the real heyday for this was during the previous decades. The reason they were so sought after was to build a kerty (carty) or as the older generation called it, a 'piler'. Some boy's efforts were real heaps of junk and shouldn't have been on the road having obviously failed their MOTs. My old man though had lived through the kerty generation and was a real enthusiast and as I've said, he was also a real DIY expert. He built me the equivalent of a kerty Ferrari. It was a total babe magnet but I was too young to understand what a babe magnet was and take advantage of the extra attention. I was ten years old and too busy cruising the streets to worry about babes.

What set it apart from other heaps of junk was the striking orange bodywork done in orange gloss paint. It looked sleek and immaculate and had class written all over it. The spacious seating area and state-of-the-art steering column and greenie line handle were of the latest design but the most unique feature and envy of all other kerty owners was the brake. This was a big stick with a piece of rubber attached which, when pushed, simply rubbed against the large back wheel and brought the kerty to a smooth stop. Or that's how my old man sold it to me!

My mate Geordie and I took it out for its first test-drive, relishing the prospect of steering such a magnificent piece of carpentry.

'Wahr ir yih waant tih go?' asked Geordie excitedly. Without any hesitation I said, 'Itz got tih be the Burnie Brae! Wull open it up an see wut this baby kin dae eh?'

'Great choice!' This was the same steep brae we used so extensively to sledge down in winter as it offered exhilarating speeds. The minor crash we had on the way to the brae should have served as a wee reminder of what we were getting into but the wind was in our sails and there was no holding back.

'Right, ehl hae furst shot cause itz mine an meh old man buhlt it.' Geordie was probably glad of my selfish attitude and no doubt quietly thought to himself as he looked down the steep slope, 'Thank Christ fir that! Ehl see how yih git on furst.'

'Right, geeza good shove.' That he did and off I trundled. In the space of five seconds I was out of control and getting faster and faster.

'Right, dinna panic,' I thought. 'Jist push the brake an wull glide tih a smooth an controlled halt. *WULL EH FUCK!'* I would have been as well rubbing chip pan oil on my palm and grabbing the wheel for all the good it was going to do. As I approached critical speed the kerty hit a little dip and before you could shout 'OH KEECH!' my vehicle had flipped upside down then, after throwing me out, had very generously decided to land on my nut. I was screaming in pain while Geordie just rolled about laughing at my misfortune. Predictably, he declined the offer of 'second go' and so we trudged back home, me to lick my wounds and ram the kerty as far up my old man's arse as it would go and Geordie to think of a less dangerous mate to go about with.

A few things have changed for the better on our scheme streets. One is that there is a hell of a lot less dog shite on them. Certainly, the invention of little green bags to pick the shite up with and carry to a designated bin has helped greatly. I do find this shift in culture extremely amusing especially when you see a very attractive lady bending down to pick up the steaming hot jobbie and walk about with it – not very glamorous although I'm not knocking it because as I said, the streets are a whole lot cleaner. Something which seems to have just disappeared without any logical explanation is white dog shite. There used to be loads of the dry white crumbly turds lying about but it's clearly retro and not very fashionable for dogs to drop any more.

Another contributing factor to the cleaner streets is definitely the removal of stray dogs. As a bairn I remember large packs of aggressive dogs terrorizing the schemes. What I didn't realise at the time was that they weren't just roaming around like some marauding canine gang looking to attack wee laddies and lassies. No, they were in heat and absolutely gagging for a shag and each member of this mob was vying for the lone female's attention whom they were all chatting up with some barking sweet talk.

Eventually, some lucky mutt would jump in there while the rest were arguing to see who was going where in the queue. His bliss turned to sheer embarrassment shortly afterwards though when he acrobatically became entangled and both dogs became joined together at the arse and facing in opposite directions. The other dogs would just rip the pish out of him with sarcastic barks and watch as some old woman came out of her house with a bucket of freezing cold water to throw over the amorous couple and split the shenanigans up. When I was younger I used to think this was some strange new breed of super dog, it was bizarre.

A couple of the pastimes we indulged in back then have disappeared into obscurity now which is maybe just as well given the highly sensitive nature of participating in them. Nowadays 'bird-nesting' and 'bee-catching' would be unconditionally frowned upon by the politically correct brigade. Our crimes against the birds and the bees populations were wholly unintentional. We merely saw them as another way of having some innocent fun and increasing our knowledge of the surrounding wildlife and nature in general, albeit in an unorthodox manner.

The term 'bird-nesting' was the name we gave to the art of collecting bird's eggs from their nests. We'd be delving into hedges, climbing trees, searching riverbanks and fields alike in search of these nests. Some boys took it really seriously and had huge collections in flat boxes which were all carefully cushioned by cottonwool or sawdust with each one named. These lads were real hardcore enthusiasts who owned detailed books on Britain's birds and would go to extraordinary lengths to add a new egg to their collections. For most of us though who had more modest collections, it was all about the adventure and the banter. The first egg in nearly everyone's shoebox display was the blackbird's egg. They were ten-a-penny with some hedges turning into overcrowded blackbird ghettos they were so abundant. Many of their eggs ended up being taken for the hell of it just to throw at a wall or at a bus. Their numbers must have declined horrendously as every hedge you saw seemed to have some scheme boy's legs dangling out of them.

The number of eggs in the nests of different species varied considerably and the general rule was that whoever spotted it (the nest) got first egg, then the second man got second and so on, that's if there *were* any more. Soon enough you were learning about the living habitats of yellowhammers, mallard ducks, wrens, the lot! First man in would stick his hand in the nest and would sometimes get a real fleg (fright) when he startled the poor bird who was still sitting there quite the thing, minding its babies. Then *BANG!* In came a dirty, faking hand to turn the place upside down with a bit of pillaging and robbing. If he was up a tree and there were eggs in the nest, he would carefully place them in his mouth and slowly climb down, taking great care not to crack them in his mouth. I must admit though, I never saw anyone try this with a couple of swan's eggs. They would have needed a mouth the size of a hippo's! You then had to 'bla' (blow) the egg and this was done by piercing a little pinhole in each end then blowing the yolk out. If the chick was beginning to form then there was no way on Earth that it was going to be blown through this tiny hole.

'Gie's that peen ower here tull eh mak twa holes.'

'Ir yih jist gonna bla thum here?'

'Eh.' You knew that you had a problem though when you were blowing for any length of time and nothing was happening or a gooey, bloody mess seaped out.

'Uhl bet its gugget!'

'Thatz wut it'll be. It'll hae a yunky in it!'

Sure enough on closer inspection you'd notice a young bird was developing inside. There was nothing else for it but to discard the egg. One of the daftest things I recall was, after realising one of the eggs was gugget, someone would say, 'Right, gie's the ither eggs an ehl pit thum back in the nest fir the mither tih sit back doon on.' As if the bird was going to be hanging about waiting on any returns?

I had a mate called Alan who was an unbelievable climber and fearless with it. On one occasion we ventured up to a rookery on the outskirts of Whitfield to get some rook's or crow's eggs. The trees were easily fifty feet high and looked terribly intimidating from the ground. Alan took off up one of these monsters like a monkey while I struggled desperately up another like a sloth wearing wellies. At the top the wind was causing the thin branches to move slightly more than I would have liked and the ground seemed a long, long way down. I was shitting myself! I held on for dear life while I thrust my hand up and into the large nest. The feeling that greeted me made me jump and just about threw me into an involuntary base jump without a parachute. Three or four little beaks pecked excitedly as they mistook my fingers for the fattest worms they'd ever seen. It was a close shave indeed.

Another time, Alan and I embarked on a more adventurous excursion and hopped on a bus for the town of Arbroath. This place is only about fifteen miles up the east coast from Dundee and is famous for the 'Arbroath Smokies'. It is also, allegedly, the capital of 'Seagull Land' and holds around ninety percent of the seagull population for the whole of Europe. These airborne 'Arbroath rats' are responsible for most of the bird 'emulsion' which lands on cars from villages like Newtyle to cities as far off as Madrid. Our plan was to hit the cliffs and bag a varied selection of their eggs. These of course were the days when they still lived near the sea and hadn't all migrated to Dundee. Cretins! We reached the top of these huge cliffs at which point I peered shakily over and down to the rocks and the sea far below.

'Fuck that Al! Thirz nae danger ehm climbin doon there, no even fir geese thit huv laid a load o golden eggs!'

'Ach awa yih poofter,' replied my mate and off he descended down a face which wouldn't have looked out of place on K2! He was out of site and gone for ages and I was beginning to think the worst when his familiar napper peeped over the lip of the cliff.

'Wahr the hell huv yih been? Ehv been worried seek! Eh thought yih wir dade!'

'Wahr dih yih think uhv been? Here, check this lot oot!' He took off this old lobster pot which he'd ingeniously made into a rucksack and revealed a brilliant haul of gull's eggs. 'No bad eh?' he said, smiling broadly. 'Although they fulmers wir a but o a nightmare, spittin this stinkin bile at is!'

The boy was a genius, far too advanced for his years. His brain seemed to need constant stimulation and he was always looking to build and make things. His parents must have noticed this creative streak he had and bought him one of those home chemistry sets. Unfortunately, one of his home-made experiments got out of control and he set his bedroom curtains on fire. Thankfully it was brought under control before the house went ablaze.

Catching bees on the other hand was a sport tackled from the safety of terra firma with no dangerous climbing involved at all. The only real hazard it carried was getting stung. All you needed to get started was a clean, empty jar with a lid on it.

This was pierced with little holes to allow your pets to breathe then you simply went out into the garden and hung about near some flowers. You soon got to know what kind they preferred. The grassy playing field in Fintry Primary School was covered in clover leafs (which we called honey) and was a hive of activity for catching bees. Your timing had to be spot on because one wrong move and you were faced with a severely pissed off bumblebee. When you'd caught a couple of these bumblers you'd watch them buzzing about and adapting to their new home so you quickly removed the lid ever so slightly and dropped a few clover flowers in to 'feed them'. You could just imagine one bumbler saying to the other, 'Did you oarder that grub?'

'Nah, no me mate. Ken wut? Ehm no that hungry anyweh.'

'Dih yih hink eel lit wih oot?'

'Well eh hope so, ehv stull got twa bags o pollen tih collect an if ehm late back tih the hev the Queen'll go right aff ir nut. Shiz a right moanin pus!'

'Eh oorz is the same mate – a total screamer! Itz *us* thitz daein ah the work tae! An fir wut? So she kin git ir leg ower an keep layin eggs. Itz bang oot o oarder!'

'Thir nivir happy ir the? Christ itz a but hot in here is it? Oh, wait a minute, there's the raif turnin. The boy's seen sense at last.'

'Aw yiv got tih be jokin! Mair boadeez comin in – an ane o thumz *ginger*!'

You'd keep filling up the jar and all the while keep gener-ously dropping in more 'grub' until it was just one big heaving mass of clover leafs and bees' faces squashed against the clear glass. Condensation would form on the inside through lack of oxygen and the bees' fur would be dripping with sweat. In our young minds we couldn't understand how they all just died especially after showing such kindness and feeding them so well. You'd lose patience with their motionless display and empty the whole lot out onto the grass in disgust. Sometimes you'd catch a bumbler and a wasp and encourage them to have a scrap. Again, you couldn't understand how they weren't tearing lumps from each other and letting go with a few stings. Even after shaking the jar rigorously they just couldn't be cajoled into setting about each other and you were left with no option but to execute them both for a pish poor show.

As you progressed in your career you realised there were loads of different kinds of bees. Some were the bog-standard yellow and black stripey kind, others were all black with a red or orange arse, some carried little orange buckets on their thighs and some were ginger. I often wondered if all the different squads stuck together and ganged up on the gingers just because the colour of their fur. They must have been indigenous Scottish bees.

My favourite bees by far were the ones we called 'yellow noseys' for the obvious reason, they had a furry yellow nose. Something which has intrigued me in later life is the fact that this particular bee had three different names within Dundee alone. It seems that towards the east where I lived, it was called a yella nosey. To the north of the city they called it a 'cannie Annie' and over in the west it was known as a 'fogey' (not to be confused with an old person!). These were the only bees we knew of that didn't sting you and what we'd do was catch them in our hands then remove their wings so we could keep them as pets. Before the politically correct among you start throwing tantrums we *did* release them back into the wild at the end of the day although I suppose they must have struggled to get back to their hives without any wings.

Wasps were a different kettle of insects altogether. I believe they were put on this Earth to annoy the hell out of us humans. Like midges, there is just no logical reason for their existence on this planet other than to cause mayhem at barbecues and picnics. During the months of August and September it's literally impossible to eat a piece on jam in the backies without getting into a fight with a mob of them. My gran Clark had the right idea and used to fill an empty jam jar with water and leave a thin skimming of jam on the rim. The wasps' greed would get the better of them as they tore in about the jam before falling arse over tit and into the jammie grave.

In Fintry my gran's house had these little air vents around the bottom and the wasps would build their bikes in them. As soon as we learned of these illegal bike-assembling factories we'd get long twigs and sticks and poke the hell out of them until they got well riled. It was great fun and worth getting a sting or two. One of the best laughs ever was when we'd collect a load of wasps and bees in a jar then go into a closie and chickenelly their door. At that point you'd give the jar a good shake to get the insects riled and mad then open the the lid in time for the house owners answering their door. You couldn't run for laughing thinking of them wrestling with a mob of angry wasps!

As the title of this chapter says, we were often 'Up Tih Nae Gade' – which in its English form translates into 'up to no good'. I'm sure the wasps, bees, birds, etc. would all agree we were just that and they must have been mighty happy when we matured slightly and moved onto some of the more conventional hobbies such as gang-fighting, watching United or Dundee from the terraces and chasing lassies.

19

YOUTHFUL DREEMZ IN HOOSIN SKEEMZ

And that folks really brings us to the end of my retro ramblings and gibberings about a time when fun was gathered by the bucket load and swallowed greedily. A time when 'political' and 'correctness' were just two big words and had never been used in the same sentence. When freedom, adventure and exploration knew no boundaries no matter how young you were.

The real enjoyment in writing this book for me personally has been the opportunity to delve back into my past and re-live the many colourful moments of my early years. I doubt very much if there would have been enough words to fill even a page had it not been for the many wonderful members of my family and friends who played starring roles (and continue to), making it a story worth telling.

I think it's true that when you get to a certain age you begin to look back fondly at the days when you were most happy and for the majority of us it is the time when we were kids and didn't have a care in the world. I can't see past the 1970s. For me the decade had the lot – the ever-changing fashions, music, burgeoning youth culture, football terraces, toys, sweets – the list goes on. Arguably, it was the last real decade of total freedom before the cotton wool 'smothering' brigade appeared to tell us 'YOU CAN'T!' Sod them I say, and a big fat 'Harvey

Smith' to them all! If I'm guilty of being stuck in the mists of nostalgia then I'll happily walk to the gallows and swing.

Indeed, if the 1st of January 1970 was about to dawn again tomorrow I'd be doing cartwheels right now although I'd probably have a certain female Prime Minister banished from the decade and transported back to the medieval days. Seriously though, it was great fun phoning my mum and dad to talk over all the little details of what we got up to and also talking to numerous friends and family about our exploits. I know for a fact that when my parents read this I'll be getting a cuff or two and possibly even a wahlup then sent to my room!

Those were the days of our lives – happy days on the streets of Dundee. We had youthful dreams in our housing schemes. It was and is – Skeem Life!